The Downward Climb

Beyond Survival of
Serial Infidelity

By Mary Banker Harpt

Prologue by Beth Johnson

Dedicated to the wonderful people who have greatly impacted my life and my living:

Beth, an angel at my prison gate and the headlamp lighting the way on the downward climb.
My three children, my three best friends.
The Six plus Five, whom I love to pieces.
My mother and father and my brother and sister: the family that spoiled me happy.
Other friends and family who encouraged me and made it safe for me to tell my story.

CONTENTS

ACKNOWLEDGMENTS

I would like to thank my CreateSpace Project Team for editing and designing the interior and cover for *The Downward Climb*. I am very grateful for their outstanding support and availability, as well as their creative, technical, and professional insight.

Capture Photography, www.capturephotography.us, provided my picture on the back cover. It has always been a pleasure to work with Capture, a company that exceeds my expectations for creativity, quality, and service.

DISCLAIMERS

Except in the case of the author and clinical psychologist, pseudonyms were used in the stories included here in *The Downward Climb*.

In brief episodes of this journey, expletives were used.

INTRODUCTION OF
DR. BETH JOHNSON

Dr. Beth Johnson is a licensed clinical psychologist and founder of Lakefront Wellness Center where she has practiced for over a decade. The Lakefront Wellness Center employs eleven clinicians who specialize in spiritual integration and mental health wellness. Dr. Johnson is a professional speaker and supervises other professionals seeking to approach mental health holistically.

PROLOGUE

I would like to take this opportunity to introduce Mary to you. I have always believed that God sends me each client and that every person I work with, teaches me something. I am certain that Mary is someone that God sent me and she has enriched my life more than she knows. Her natural demeanor is bubbly and outgoing. She has always been kind and loving in her relationship with me; and from all that I can tell, with others. If you met her, you would like her and be put at ease by her. She looks for strengths in others and is always quick to point them out. She has a grateful and hardworking nature. She is a survivor and a giver. There have been a few times she has brought tears to my eyes when I saw the kindness and compassion in her mothering. Though our relationship has been only a professional one, one day I would hope to call her friend. Having said all of this, part of our work together was to push past the outer exterior of being good natured and show the world her darker side, her pain side, and her anger. This book does that well. Be ready for some curse words and jokes about sex. Her personality is thoroughly enjoyable in person and in her book.

Mary has trusted her life and inner world to me and out of my professional protectiveness I would like to share some of my protective thoughts with her readers. Foremost is that Mary has completely opened the most shameful and painful memories of her former marriage to you, the reader, for the purpose of offering you company in whatever type of emotional pain that you are in. She truly desires to communicate to you that you are not alone, and she breaks her forty year silence to bring the topic of infidelity and emotional abuse out in the open. In her story you will possibly be shocked by her denial, naiveté and the manner in which she dealt with her husband's blatant display of affection for other women. It is my request to you as a reader that you withhold judgments and criticisms and truly observe with sensitivity the unfolding that occurs throughout the book.

In the beginning stages of the book you observe her in a more emotionally disconnected state from the trauma. She begins the book with a snapshot of her "Beaver Cleaver" upbringing to give you a frame of reference for her naiveté. As the book (and therapy) progressed, her insight, pain and process become clearer. It truly was a testimony of her strength as well as weakness that she kept these things secret, even from herself. How strong she must have been to hold onto love and marriage under those circumstances. She gathered no support in order to protect her husband and family; yet how weak she was as an advocate for her own needs. The process of telling her own secrets, even to herself, was a painful journey; and she often writes in her book the shame responses that occurred at the computer when she acknowledged for the first time all that she had unconsciously stored in her memory. Please, be gentle with her in your appraisal! Denial is a powerful survival strategy. Some humans come more equipped to use it than others. Mary was quite adept with denial; but in her recovery, she boldly faces all and asks for more.

Mary took great risk to come out with her story, but I know that she did so out of an earnest desire for Christians to be able to come forward on this issue and any issue of shame, whether they are the victim or perpetrator. She despises the effects of Christian judgment on our ability to be supportive when we are in ugly circumstances. One of Mary's first therapy lessons that she took to heart in a manner that I had never observed before, was "Insert yourself!" It was an observation I made that her fears and temperament kept her from using her gifts and making an impact where she could. She digested this lesson and almost immediately started disclosing her secret to friends and family. The impact was startling to her: people were helped when she inserted herself. Everywhere people are hurting in silence and in shame because we are afraid to speak out our own pain. Mary vowed to not be afraid to insert herself. The book is the masterpiece of that lesson. She is now inserting herself in a public way and she has no control over the outcomes.

The book is based on her memory, *her perceptions*, and our processing of trauma in psychotherapy. We do not claim to have arrived at perfect conclusions nor have we finished working at the time of the book's publication. There may be better alternative therapeutic interpretations or guidance. We do not claim expertise; we only expose a process and a journey for the reader's benefit. We acknowledge that her exposure may bring emotional harm in the future to herself and others who are part of this story. To those that may be offended or hurt by the book, that is not her intent. She is making a conscious choice to offer her story and accept the consequences; so that others may be helped and so that she is true to herself.

Mary offers my assessment of her ex-husband in the book, someone I have never met. This is not an uncommon process in therapy. Therapists assess family members without meeting them through their clients' perceptions. We do try to bear in mind that perceptions are not necessarily reality. I acknowledge that my opinions of her ex-husband are only opinions and may be lacking in foundation because I have never met him. Mary uses my descriptor of him "polygamist" not literally, as he was only married to one wife; but as an emotional descriptor. This book is not about revenge; it is a story of forgiveness and recovery. *It is her story to tell.*

Finally, there is a strong Christian message but happily, she doesn't hide the ugliness of sin nor does she always "toe the line" so to speak as a Christian. She is comfortable with the gray areas of divorce and is incensed with Christian judgment when it keeps people from reaching out. She is an advocate for compassion, mercy, and forgiveness. She loves unconditionally and wants to bring that message forward rather than portraying the perfect Christian message that passes the test of legalism. The message is about her own struggle with sin, her own self-loathing, and ultimately grace for herself. In sum, GRACE is prioritized before RULES of right and wrong. If you are a Christian, looking for perfection in her presentation of her story, you will be disappointed. If you are looking for someone who is real and compassionate, full of grace and kindness, Mary is your girl. YOU GO GIRL!

Beth Johnson

I

THIS IS WHERE THE STORY BEGINS

SPOILED HAPPY

It was Buck Night at the drive-in movies, a family night for the five of us. Jerry, Jan, and I were young kids in the back seat of the family car—a Buick, of course. Dad had built a wooden platform over the back seat, so we could sit or lie down quite comfortably at the drive-in or on long trips up north. It was summertime in the 1950s, and life was happy.

The three of us would help Mom make popcorn and line up Graf's sodas for each of us. Root beer and orange were my favorites. Mom poured the warm, buttered and salted popcorn into a blue-and-white metal container with bold print: *Jay's Potato Chips.* We all carried something out to the car, including our jackets in case it was cool outside when we played on the playground in front of the big, outdoor screen.

Dad drove to the theatre and rolled down the window to hand the guy at the ticket booth a dollar bill. He would always search for a good spot in a good row so all of us could see the screen clearly. He pulled the car up to the speaker post, grabbed the silver speaker, checked the sound, and hooked it up on his window.

"Can we go to the swings, Mom?"

"That's fine. Stick together."

We would. We three had fun together. Jerry was three years older than I; Jan, two years older. Yep, I was the youngest, and I was spoiled happy. All three of us were.

The drive-in ads came up on the screen first, and then we three Knuckleheads (as Dad called us) ran back to the car. A bunch of cartoons and two movies, maybe westerns or Disney flicks, would be the order of the evening. All was a pretty sweet deal for just a "buck." But my favorite part was the drive home after a great family night. We kids would be curled up or stretched out in the back seat. Mom and Dad would talk softly.

I coughed. Mom turned her head.

"You okay, Bug?" Dad asked.

"Uh-huh." I closed my eyes and started to doze again. I still remember the soft sound of the blinker as we made the last right turn onto our block.

I smiled a little kid's sleepy smile. I knew I was loved. I knew I was valued. I knew I was safe. I was home. I was spoiled happy.

But I didn't always feel that way. When I was eighteen going on nineteen, things changed. That was when "spoiled happy" was introduced to the "hurt deeply" of adversity. When I was in high school, I fell in love. I got married when I had just turned nineteen. The adversity of adulthood pounded me through my twenties. I got divorced at thirty-one. But Mary-spoiled-happy wouldn't share the stories of Mary-hurt-deeply.

Forty years after my initiation into hardship at eighteen, my life was about to be shaken up just enough to require me to revisit my hidden stories of adversity. After many years of not dating, I was fifty-eight and wanted to find "Mr. Right." I had retired from my memorable and rewarding twenty-two-year career with the YMCA, climbed Mt. Kilimanjaro, completed my master's degree, and was enjoying two part-time jobs. My own three Knuckleheads were now out of college and married. I call them "The Three," and they are indeed my three best friends.

Since I wanted to get married again, I made a significant investment into a dating service. The relationship consultant and saleswoman said,

"Just think—all the men who join *Happily Ever After with the Woman/Man of Your Dreams* pay this much too, because they want to find wives as much as you want to snag a husband." Those who learned I had joined a dating service were surprised that I wanted to date and marry again. I had tried some of the dating websites; many do find a heartthrob that way, but it didn't happen for me.

The first guy I met online magically fell in love with me after a handful of emails. He contacted me before a trip to Guyana and then emailed me upon his arrival. Lo and behold, he told me he had dropped his laptop and desperately needed me to send him one so he could carry on with his diamond trading. I ran right out to Best Buy, bought a sweet laptop and shipped it on the spot. I'm kidding. I'm kidding! I cancelled all of my online dating website subscriptions and got a cat. (His name is Gideon, and he is adorable.)

So here I was, meeting the first of twenty-four referrals in a contract service that was way-over-the-top too expensive. What was I thinking? I dated Ted, the third referral, for a while. I believed his stories of financial hardship, including the one where he went bankrupt trying to pay his deceased mother's hospital bills. I really thought he was genuine. He said, "I won't be able to pay you back until June." Disregarding my intuition and a still, small voice, I trusted him and loaned him a significant sum. As I continued to date him, I caught on to his manipulative tendencies. There were way too many red flags. I saw how he treated others, family and friends. I learned from his friends and family that manipulation and lying were his trademarks and that his mode of interacting with people was to use them. No, he never paid me back, and I am quite sure he never will. At one time he told me, "You know we will disappoint each other." He used that statement as a wild card to break promises. The sound of it was all too familiar.

Ted's scam actually had a higher price tag than the con of the "laptop sting" guy. The dating website con artist had known what he was about, but this "you're-the-best-woman-I-ever-met" guy was in total denial of his warped way of interacting with people. I discovered that he had lied about everything. Somewhere along his road of life, his handle on truth and honesty had fallen down a deep, dark hole. If he doesn't get help, he will eventually trip and fall in himself.

LATE-NIGHT EMAIL: CLICK SEND

A fuller recognition of Ted's betrayal and the next dating experience brought me to a point of truth. Our first date was dinner at a very yummy pizza place. I had arrived first. In this particular dating program, you don't know what your date looks like until you meet. When "Bob," my date, stepped into the restaurant, I couldn't tell if he was pleased with what he saw or not. He was six foot two and very handsome. *Hmm.*

We talked a lot. He said, "You know, I am usually pretty shy, but you are so easy to talk to." It was snowing lightly outside when he walked me to the car and said, "We should get together again." Ah, yes, I've heard that before. I had learned from a few dates already that even at this age, the guy in the dating scene might not mean what he says. "I'll give you a call" means "nice to meet you, but there is no way I'll be calling you anytime soon." I liked Bob, but did not expect him to call me. He didn't. I requested another dating referral.

A month later, Bob did call. Now, just what does calling a month later mean in the over-the-hill-and-beyond dating scene? He asked me out, and we went to a Thursday-night movie—*The King's Speech.* Early in the movie, he took my hand and rested it on his thigh. *Hmm.* At one point, I pulled my hand away for some reason and then later walked it back under his hand. It was nice to feel his manly quads. *Hmmm.*

As you probably know, the movie was incredible. We went to Applebee's for a late dinner and talked until midnight. He listened intently as I shared my testimony of faith with him. Bob walked me to my car. I felt like a young high-school girl. "I wonder if he is going to draw close to me. I wonder if he might even kiss me." We reached the car and walked to the driver's side. As I pressed the unlock button, I asked, "So, are we getting together again?"

He got closer and I looked up at him. "What do you think?" he said with a warm and very handsome smile.

I looked up at his face and thought, *Ooh! I want to kiss those lips.* So I did. *Hmmmm.*

I slid into the car and pulled out of the parking lot. Fifty-eight and back in high school. What fun.

We dated a few more times. He would sometimes seem close and as if he wanted to be with me, while at other times he would withdraw. He likes me, he likes me not. He didn't call for a while. Then on February 14th he called and said, "I just wanted you to know, it's Valentine's Day and I am thinking about you. What are you doing this week? Are you busy, or do you have some time for me in there?" I told him I could go out Friday or Saturday night, perhaps both. He said, "Well, no."

I was confused. Well, I was confused until a few weeks later, when my cell phone rang in the school parking lot after my young granddaughter's basketball game (which was great fun to watch, by the way). It was Bob. I was hoping it would be. I had texted him the day before: "So, will I have a hot date with a hot and gorgeous guy on Saturday night?"

Bob's response was not what I expected, though. He said, "I'm not doing anything tonight, but I don't want to see you." That was just how he said it. He said it a number of times. He was just being honest. I'm glad, but once was enough, thank you very much.

He had different religious and doctrinal views and assumed my political views were of a certain bent. His concern about our differences appeared to be growing. In more ways than one, he had told me, "You're such a wonderful person. You're smart and sweet and you always put other people before yourself. And you're pretty. You would make any man's life better. But if you were the woman for me, all this other stuff would not matter." It was as if he were trying to convince himself.

I told him I had to go. I could not hear it anymore. I was in my car in the parking lot. Other cars were around, but they were empty. I was alone. I cried. I didn't intend to, but I cried one of those short-but-hard cries. Feeling this depth of sorrow was an unexpected, spontaneous response. The disappointment had unearthed trauma buried many years ago. I had been planning to go to the YMCA to work out after my granddaughter's game and told myself I was still going to do that. I needed to work out. I rode the stationary bike for an hour or so. I rode hard and just kept my eyes closed. It was as if no one else were there, just me and the bike. I didn't want to see or talk to anyone, especially if I started crying again. On the way home, I stopped to grab a bottle of merlot. I planned to drink the whole thing, and I did. It was very late on a Saturday night; I sent a message to the Three—my three kids. The subject line was "Being Known." Sending a totally unexpected email late at night after drinking a bottle of good wine is usually not a good idea and is potentially hazardous. Once you click SEND, there is no getting it back. The message is out there.

My oldest daughter read it and tried to call me. She told me later that she came over to my house to see if I was okay. When she saw me moving in the large picture window, she felt reassured that I was all right. She texted her brother and sister to warn them that the email was awful and that they might not want to read it.

It was a very hard email to read. I didn't want it to be. It wasn't a message one would normally send via email. It was a tough message. I had protected my children from knowing the story for decades; I had protected my ex, as I had always done. This new experience of rejection had led to an unexpected reawakening of the trauma of serial infidelity

I had experienced in my marriage. I did not intend, by any means, to step back into the past. I had tried to silence my emotional disturbance by working out hard and drinking a bottle of merlot, but the bottled grapes loosened the lockdown I had on being vulnerable and liberated me to reveal just a fraction of my story in an email that told of the beginning of "Mary-hurt-deeply" and just one or two of her deepest wounds.

The next morning, my daughter called me. We talked for a while and then she asked, *Mom, did you ever share what you went through when you were married to Dad?*

"No. I never told anyone." For forty years I had kept everything to myself. I protected him. I protected the kids. No one knew my story.

Mom, you have to tell someone every fucking detail. You have to share it with someone who can help you in this. You have to share it with someone who is a professional and understands how to help you. My daughter loves me a lot. She is one of my dearest friends. In a caring, wise, loving, and gently direct way, she continued to talk with me on the phone.

I remember crying, "He never said he was sorry!"

I knew she was right. I didn't know who I should seek out to help me. I knew a psychiatrist, a good friend who had helped me deal with depression a few years before. I had told him at that time that I was "in a different place," an emotional place where I was feeling down and irritable, and I had no idea why. He truly helped me a lot. I was very grateful. By this time, when I was at a new crossroads, he had concluded his private practice and was serving in a hospital more than full time. In addition, I felt I would be most comfortable with a female specialist at this intersection of past and present. My daughter mentioned the name of a psychologist she knew. *"You will like her personality and you will like her as a person. She is very professional."*

I called Dr. Beth and left her a message that I had hit a wall, a dark wall. I needed help. She responded.

LOVE NOTES FOR MY JOURNEY

When I began this journey into the long-lost forever of my past, I remembered the lovely and encouraging messages from my children after my late-night email to them:

From: Katy Date: 6 March 2011 03:01

Subject: Re: Being Known

To: Mary Banker Harpt <mharpt@familymail.com

Cc: her sister Joy and her brother John

Mom,

First, thank you for sending us this letter. I am not afraid of hearing this part of your story. I think that the conversation that we had at the Coastlight Hotel at Kusadasi, prepared me a bit.

Thank you for protecting us in our young years from some of these things. . .But thank you too for letting it out now so we can know more of the life of our mom - our strong amazing mother who loves us so and never deserved to be hurt as she was.

Next, I am sooo sorry that you went through so much alone. That the amazing experience of bringing three children into the world that you love so much and we know it, also had such painful near despair threads weaved through that tapestry that will always be there.

As these threads, threads that were always there, are standing out right now. . .mom I do not think it is for nothing. I think, and hope, that the Spirit is bringing you to a "wall"—this dark night that, though it is so dark right now and so difficult, you are going to go through and be who He is making you to be on the other side.

These are such deep, painful parts of your life, Mom. We support you in this tender time.

We love you,

Katy

She sent a second email a few minutes later:

From: Katy

Date: 6 March 2011 03:08

Subject: a few other thoughts

To: Mary Banker Harpt < mharpt (@)familymail.com>

Cc: Joy and John

Mom,

I wanted to write these few other thoughts separate from the other email as they are ideas and did not merit being a response to your tender email.

This is such a deep time of dealing with these very painful threads in your life. I think it would be so good to see a professional counselor/psychologist on a regular basis to hash them out. They are not things to be hashing out alone. Someone you can just really feel so free to tell the whole story to, someone who knows maybe what questions to ask and who has experience. Do you know a counselor you trust? I could find some names if you want from Tom Walters. He knows a lot of professional counselors probably who are great as he is one himself. What do you think?

As far as this other Bob——(not sure if I am missing the boat here or if this is not good advice so take it with a grain of sea salt and pepper). From the beginning he seemed more of a hesitant guy, so cautious and what not. While you are feeling sad about this situation, and so you should, please do not let yourself feel rejected from him. Maybe it is allowing some of this much deeper rejection to come to the surface, the intense rejection that wants dealing with. Be sad about him, but don't take on the feeling of rejection from him——he is not worth it. Not that he is to blame, but he just does not have the right to have a piece of your tender heart right now. Let him go——he is just a guy, though kind and interesting maybe, looking to meet people and probably not sure what he wants.

I love you sooo.

Katy

In many conversations my daughter Joy offered heartfelt, reassuring concern; compassion, advice, and encouragement; as well as her wise guidance and great strength. It was a great gift to me, especially when she said: *Mom, this is all part of your journey.*

About a year or so before my over-the-top email, when I was beginning my older adult adventures in dating, Joy had said: *Mom, we all aspire to be like you. You made a new life for yourself. You ran one of the biggest YMCAs in the country. You're an athlete. You did triathlons and you climbed Mt Kilimanjaro. You lift weights and you were a strength training coach. You are a scholar and a writer. You are a* world traveler. You are a chaplain and a missionary. And you're a theologian for heaven's sake. You care about people and always give them the benefit of the doubt. You think the best of them. People are attracted to you.

When I introduced my children to a guy I had met, Joy told me later: *He is a nice guy. We like him, but he has lived his life so small. Your world is so much bigger. I sometimes think I need to be your dating coach.*

One September a number of years ago, our family was up North for an off-road bike race. The whole gang was all packed into the car and ready to head out; John was in the driver's seat. As he watched me, the last one out of the cabin door, double—well, maybe triple-checking— whether I had locked it for sure, he said, *Mom, when I grow up, I want to be just like you.* He was a twenty-five-year-old with a wife and daughter. I laughed at myself and his comment. It was hilarious.

I recall another time when my son was about fifteen and we had just gotten into the car so I could drive him to school. I had shared something with him about work or whatever, and he responded with wise, thought-ful, insightful comments. I said, "Thanks, John. That was really discern-ing and helpful." I was really impressed.

Mom, we are just giving back what you put into us.

When my son was in high school and the girls were home from col-lege, the four of us were sitting around our dining room table one day. I shared, "You know, there were times when I let go of my right to assert myself as so often your dad was insisting on having it his way while you guys were growing up. I let it go because I didn't want you to be in be-tween and forced to choose: listen to Dad or listen to Mom. I didn't want you to be stuck in the middle of such a dilemma."

My son put his hand on my shoulder. *You have no idea how much that helped.*

A Mother's Day card my son wrote on May 10, 2009, read:

From playing basketball with me in the driveway at the house, to letting me ride my bike next to you while you run, to the times I snuck out to scare you while you were walking to the car, to kayaking and biking in Door County, to mountain biking at John Muir and Chequamegon, to our trip to Arizona *(every inch of it)*, and to *you being a wonderful grandma to my girls, I have and always will feel honored to call myself your son. There is no mom more fun and loving than you. You take the cake and I thank you for always being there for me. Words cannot express the love I feel for my Mom!*

Thanks and I love you, John.

This email John sent on May 23, 2011:

Mom, we all love you. And Christ is the only friend that can give you the comfort and peace that you are looking for. Look to him and give him your anguish. He will carry it.

My response was, "Thanks John! You are so very right!! Wow, what a great son you are!"

He sent back: *And what a great mom you are! If only the rest of the world were so lucky to have such a dedicated and selfless mom. You are an inspiration and I know God has great things yet for you. Stand strong Mom. We are all behind you.*

Joy left these encouraging words on my answering machine after my retirement party, Thursday, January 25, 2007 at 8:08 p.m.:

Hi, Mom, it's me. I am sorry we bolted out of there. I had so much I wanted to say, but everybody wanted to say stuff to you. And just to start with, we just were talking in the car about how powerful it was that everybody—and—well the things that you wanted your life to say to people, they said before you even had to mention it. I mean your life was a testimony to them, and we know it was; but to have them articulate that before you even got up to say what it was you wanted your life to say, that's powerful. And I said to Steve that we all try to speak and minister to people in our own way, but it reminded me of a diving contest. Each different dive has a different degree of difficulty, and you choose the highest degrees of difficulty, Mom, you just verbalize it all. You put it all out there. The rest of us maybe don't take the most challenging approach to sharing our faith, but you do it and you still score 10's with people, and I just want to tell you we are so proud of you and I am so sure God is proud of you that you don't waste a word. And it really was a wonderful night. Just so proud of you, and we had so much to say and would have said it if we had had the opportunity. And we love you a lot!

Four years later, I still had her message saved on my answering machine that was still plugged in even though I didn't have a land line anymore. Leave it to God to bless me with three amazing children and a gift and love for speaking and a huge love for people. The credit belongs to him. You know it does. He answered my prayers as I asked him what to write for my retirement dinner and to guide and guard me as I spoke. I had been thinking about my retirement message for days.

On the way to campus the day before my retirement recognition dinner, I was thinking and struggling about my speech during the whole drive. Nothing was coming together in my head. I pulled into the parking lot and prayed, "Okay, God, so this is it. I want all of the people who come to my retirement party to know that they matter to you and that you love them."

"So tell them," God answered. And that is what I did.

My children are my best friends. I share these stories, a handful of moments to remember, to create a quick snapshot of their support and understanding, love and compassion. Their active and positive presence in my life, exemplified in these "love notes," permitted me to begin this journey and to take the necessary step over the edge. Together, they held the safety rope for my downward climb into the crevasse.

THE CREVASSE OF BEING KNOWN
TAKEN TO THE EDGE

In the early spring of 2006, the Six and the Four (my "six" kids—my three plus their spouses—and my four grandkids at the time), came over for a visit. After dinner, we sat in the living room of my flat. My "three sons" were sitting on the comfy leather sofa. I told them how a few friends of mine were planning a short-term mission to Sudan and then would set out to climb Mount Kilimanjaro. In unison, the three young men turned to me and said, "Mom! You can do this!" The three young women across the room responded, "Yeah, Mom!" And that is how, at age fifty-four, I began a new adventure.

My youngest daughter said she would take me out to Colorado in October to be my guide on a few climbs in Rocky Mountain National Park. You see, there was a small hitch: I had never climbed a mountain before. My son encouraged me to get back out to the Kettle Moraine and other nearby trekking places in Wisconsin to get back in shape. Once again, I became a frequent visitor at the YMCA.

For six years or so following a car accident and neck injury, I had retreated from my former workout and exercise regimens in fear of aggravating or recreating the pain that had plagued me for all that time. I remember my son saying, "I never had a fragile mom before." Ever since an amazing surgeon fused cervical vertebrae 5 and 6, I was relieved of most of the former chronic pain. Now, it was time to get strong again. And I did.

On December 19, 2006, I climbed to the "Roof of Africa." It was both beautiful and brutal. Our experienced guide from Kenya nodded his head as he pondered the moment. "Know that you have climbed Kilimanjaro at her worst." Pouring rain in the rainforest, cold and sleet in mountain tundra, snow and wind as we approached Uhuru Peak at 19,340 feet, followed by a slippery descent in torrential rains. Love note: While I was in Africa, my son changed the answering message on my home phone: "Mary is not home right now. She is in Tanzania, climbing Mount Kilimanjaro."

Summit of Kilimanjaro December 19, 2006

My children, their spouses, and my grandchildren made a red, white, and blue "summit stick" (a wooden paint stirrer) complete with their individual pictures and a short message from each of them. I carried it with me on the mountain and placed it there on The Roof of Africa.

After my summit experience, I read an account of two climbers who dared to summit the unclimbed, perilous west face of the twenty-one-thousand-foot Siula Grande in the Andes. In 1985, Joe Simpson and Simon Yates had just reached the summit when Simpson was catastrophically pitched off the vertical face of an ice ledge and broke his leg. Darkness loomed and a horrific blizzard waged war against the two climbers. Yates, desperate yet determined, tried to lower his friend to safety. Ultimately, Yates was compelled to do the unthinkable. He cut the rope, the very lifeline that harnessed Simpson's broken body. It was a drastic measure in a drastic and despairing situation, that otherwise would have claimed both of their lives. In his book, *Touching the Void*, Simpson writes about the ordeal:

The wind swung me in a gentle circle. I looked at the crevasse beneath me, waiting for me. It was big. Twenty feet wide at least. I guessed that I was hanging fifty feet above it. It stretched along the base of the ice cliff. Below me it was covered with a roof of snow, but to the right it opened out and a dark space yawned there. Bottomless, I thought idly. No. They're never bottomless. I wonder how deep I will go. To the bottom. . .to the water at the bottom? God! I hope not! (p. 107)

. . .I fell silently, endlessly into nothingness, as if dreaming of falling. I fell fast, faster than thought, and my stomach protested at the swooping speed of it. . . .I wasn't stopping, and for an instant blinding moment I was frightened. Now, the crevasse! Ahh. . .NO!! (p. 108)

The acceleration took me again, mercifully fast, too fast for the scream which died above me. . . (p. 108)

Near the end of the book, Simpson writes: *I can add only that however painful readers may think our experiences were, for me this book still falls short of articulating just how dreadful were some of those lonely days. I simply could not find the words to express the utter desolation of the experience.* (p. 206. The book is a must read; the DVD a must watch.)

Now, here I was, at the edge of a cold, dark, and deep crevasse on my own "life mountain." Once again, the Six would be my wise cheerleaders. It had not been in my plan to be at the edge of this fissure in my past. It, too, had been an experience of utter desolation. I had never seen a crevasse and was not looking forward to climbing down into it. Usually the idea is to cross over. This was *not* my design. It sounded absurd and awful, slippery and scary, dangerous and dumb.

When I first met Dr. Beth Johnson and began to share my story, she said, while looking at me with a face full of caring, concern, and gentle reflection, that in her more than twenty years of practice she had not ever heard something quite this awful. "This is not going to be easy for you. It would be easier if your ex-husband were an alcoholic and beat you every Friday or Saturday night." I knew she was right. For some reason, not quite clear to me yet, I felt required to go back.

At first, I described this journey of descent as dark. But it actually wasn't dark for me. Because I had begun to share my story, because I was encouraged to be known, it was if I now had a bright headlamp securely strapped to my forehead to illuminate the crevasse. Dr. Beth's discernment, wisdom, and compassion powered a bright lantern that would be lowered down and down to the deeper and deeper places of memory. The thoughts and prayers of the Six (and soon, other family and friends), would help sustain me in this difficult and often painful return to the deep woundedness and brokenness of my past.

After her forewarning of a painful and difficult reentry into the shadows of my past, Beth had added, "But as you blossomed once before, you will again." Even at our first meeting on my journey, I felt safe, hopeful, and sincerely validated. This was good. This might very well be one of the smartest things I had ever done.

A few days after my first session, I took Boaz, my sweet yellow Labrador, for an early-morning walk. The air was crisp; the sky, blue and beautiful. The lingering moon was huge and shining in the rising sun, glowing even. It seemed as if the moon were beaming, delighted to be brightened and warmed by the sun. Looking at the "Son," the woman in the moon was lit up to the center of herself; her face was revealed, bright, warm, and evident. Her eyes were now open but were not blinded by the light.

My initial email to my children titled "Being Known" had set in motion a journey into the long, lonely forever of my past. It was just a brief glance over the edge of the never-before-explored crevasse. I would soon become aware of the seemingly countless levels of treacherous ice I had to break through to heal. It would be a difficult downward climb.

THE CREVASSE OF BEING KNOWN
THE DOWNWARD CLIMB

I fell in love with the man who would become my husband when I was a junior in high school. He was new to our school, so I thought he was a sophomore. We were both on the Debate Team; I think that is how we met. After a while, Bob asked me to go out with him. Yes, his name also was Bob. I said no. My boyfriend at the time, Jeff, had left to go overseas as a foreign exchange student. I really missed him and hadn't let go of the relationship. Jeff wrote me regularly. In one letter, he essentially told me that he was inviting someone to a school dance there and was releasing the relationship. I was sad, but I understood. I then let myself disengage from the relationship. Bob asked me out again and I said yes. I liked him, and we continued to date. He would often express his concern that I would "dump" him when Jeff returned in our senior year. I told him I wouldn't do that, and I didn't.

I remember one date when I wore a really sweet, white, lacy dress. I could tell Bob liked it. He liked how I kissed him that night even more. I kissed him before I stepped into the house. He told me some time later that he had never been kissed like that and had thought, "Wow!"

We became good friends and spent a lot of time together researching and preparing for debate tournaments and all. He threw a surprise birthday party for me at his house. It was great fun. Many of our friends were there.

During high school, Bob worked at Robbie's, a drive-in hamburger joint, where he flipped burgers and waited on customers. He wore white jeans and a white shirt and a white paper hamburger-place hat that didn't distract from his hunkiness at all. He was standing at the drive-in window. I parked my car and walked up to the window to place my order. My then-high school sweetheart grabbed the inside top of the window frame and pulled himself through the window, feet first. As smooth as anything, there he was, standing in front of me. I actually am smiling and giggling as I write this. He looked ever so handsome and cute. What a hottie!

One winter, I had a new pair of mittens with fluorescent green and black squares and black, patent-leather straps with gold buckles at the wrist. Bob was walking me home from school, which was about two miles out of his way. He carried my tenor saxophone for me. After we said good-bye at my house, he went back toward the school and halfway there, he found one of the mittens I had unknowingly dropped. He turned around and walked back in the snow and cold to take it to me at my house. Then he walked all the way back to his home.

Bob would be upset and jealous if I talked to some guy from the band or one of my classes. I began to spend less and less time with my friends. I don't remember talking about my dreams and plans with Bob.

After our first semester of college, I sensed a change in the way Bob treated me. I can't really name what changed—it was a distancing in some ways, perhaps. During a conversation after we had just finished our first year of undergrad and before our wedding date, when we were both still eighteen, he said to me, "You know, everyone in medical school sleeps around, so it's a pretty sure thing that I will sleep around with nurses."

I didn't say anything. I couldn't respond. I didn't expect, nor was I prepared for, any such comment. What was he saying? We were in love. I loved him; he loved me. I had given all of myself to him. We were planning a wedding. I didn't know how to disengage from this relationship of young love I found myself in. Was he telling me that he actually intended to betray me? Was he simply saying, "It is what it is?" Did he mean what he was saying? At that point, I could not have told you why I was silent or why I didn't confront the situation or why I didn't just end the relationship. I had let go of all my dreams and my friends. My parents were upset that I was marrying. What happened to my high school friend and debate partner? What had changed for my high school sweetheart?

I had said nothing in response to my fiancé. The question is, then, what did I do with his statement? What did I say to myself? I told myself that other women must be prettier than me. *I am not enough for him. He will be in a different world, and I will not be a part of it. I will not be good enough for it.*

My security in the relationship was dissolved before we ever made our vows at the altar. I was not safe. Trust had been damaged. And now I wonder what he ever meant when he said, "I do." Perhaps this is where the assumed license for serial infidelity was claimed. It is where the slow destruction of my belief in my own worth began. I suppressed justifiable outrage at his intentions and turned them inward, on myself. This is where "spoiled happy" met "hurt deeply."

I got pregnant three and a half months after our wedding day, both of us just nineteen. My husband worked at a nursing home, and his schedule would have allowed him to join me at prenatal classes. I was looking forward to attending them with my husband. Right before the classes were to start, he chose to change his schedule at work. He would no longer be joining me. I asked him why; he had no explanation. I asked him to change it back. He would not. I went by myself. I was very aware of other couples laughing and giggling and having fun as they went through the exercises together. When we did floor exercises, lying on our backs, that was when I would let myself cry. It was then that no one could see my tears. No one would notice. I was all alone. It became apparent a short time later that during my pregnancy, my husband was involved with an assistant he worked with at the nursing home.

A very young African American woman was also there at the first delivery prep class. We paired up for the exercises, because we were the two who did not have partners to help us. I drove her home the night of the first class and hoped she would keep coming. I wanted to keep on encouraging her. I had the sense that she was a single mom. She did not return to the class. I was sad about that.

My husband continued his affair. He seemed embarrassed to see me and would actually ignore me when I came to the nursing home to bring him supper when he was on break. He treated me the same way when I went to see him play softball. I felt I was not pretty and not lovable. I felt alone.

Since my husband had "skipped" class, he did not know how to coach me in labor. But he held my hand, and that did help a lot. When he came to visit at the hospital, the nurse would give our sweet, tiny daughter to him and he would collapse in the hospital visitor's chair after his long and hard day. Our little sweetie would sleep packaged in his arms. He would doze off as well. He loved this sweet, precious baby. I looked on and watched happily.

My husband was faithful for a while (or more likely not, I guess) but soon there would be another affair. I would heal, feel safe, and begin to trust; then it would happen again. That was the damning part of it all… broken trust, my healing, and then broken trust again.

One evening, my husband and I went out to a favorite spot of ours for dinner. It held a romantic memory for us. It was a favorite for his mom and dad, too. Rita, his second or third mistress, was actually watching our daughter in our home. As we waited for our food, my husband talked about Rita. My happiness fled and the smile left my face.

I asked him how many times he had had sex with her. He said that he could count how many times on one hand. Translated, I guess he was saying: countless times. I was already sick at heart, and to think this comment was perhaps prepared and planned—one he thought was evasively witty—was awful. On another occasion I went to see my husband at work, and she was there. Overcome by what I now can identify as embarrassment and shame, I quickly withdrew from the room, the room full of the other EMTs, my husband, and her.

My husband told me, and I don't know why, that Rita's husband didn't want to have children. "Rita told me she wants to get pregnant, and if her husband doesn't want to, she will get pregnant with someone else." My high school sweetheart, my husband, the father of my child, said to me: "Mary, I want to be that man." I sat still in paralyzed silence. Any remaining sense of my self-worth died that day.

My husband was not expecting me to be expecting our second daughter. As he pulled his car into the lot behind our apartment building and got out of the car, I yelled from the porch of our apartment, "I'm pregnant!" He was having an affair with a new mistress from Australia at the time. I can't remember her name anymore. He was "taken aback," as people sometimes say. Sometime later, I wondered if he had been taken aback because he was planning to leave me and marry this woman from Australia. He did want to go with her on a trip to Canada.

Here is a therapy interlude. Over a year after I began my therapy and we were reviewing some of this earlier writing for my book, my psychologist and I experienced an increased awareness about the confusing scenarios of this serial infidelity. My former husband and I were living in this same apartment when he told me he wanted to have a child with Rita. This is the home where the full extent of his relationship with Rita became clear. Perhaps Rita had become a second wife figure for him and the woman from Australia was the mistress in *that* relationship. Here I thought he maybe was going to leave me and marry Miss Australia, but it was Rita he wanted to have a child with. "Australia" fit in there somewhere. He was involved with Rita and Australia at the same time, before my second daughter was born.

Ever since our first little one turned two, I had been looking forward to another little one. I was ever so happy that I was pregnant. I had always thought that it was a strong motherly instinct for me to desire another child after two years. I cannot now tell you if this desire was also influenced by my husband's expressed desire to have a child with his mistress, Rita. Did I hope he would love me and that I would be enough? How could I have? I don't know. I just don't know. He had essentially abandoned me when I was pregnant with our first child. But now he wanted to have a child with someone else.

When our second daughter was born and her father came to the hospital, he was so happy to see her. He pulled her tiny blanket back to see her fingers and count her toes. Ah, perfect as expected. He said I should stay in the hospital the full five days. My doctor had planned to send me home after three days, so I told him my husband wanted me to stay the extra days. As I look back, I am surprised the hospital didn't just ship me out. I realized later that my husband probably had his most current mistress, Australia, in our home and in our bed, while I remained in the hospital. It wasn't my well-being that he had in mind. I couldn't cry, but the sadness was deep, difficult, and disturbing. I kept it all to myself.

Once, when we were living in our second apartment on Beloit Road and my husband was not at home, my sweet first baby was sleeping in her crib in the second bedroom. I struggled with an urge to just vanish. Disappear. But not kill myself. I didn't want anyone to feel awful or sad. I just wanted to run away, far away. But my precious baby Joy was in the nursery in our home. I couldn't leave. I wouldn't leave.

At another time when we still lived in that second story apartment, I pulled my hands down the sides of my face again and again and again, pressing my fingers hard as I cried in desperation, "Why? Why? Why?" I caused some bruises on my face. I tried to hide them. My mother noticed the bruises and was worried. I told her it was nothing. I didn't know what to say.

When we moved into the flat above my folks (our third home together) before my son was conceived, I found a love letter from Rita to my husband. He had torn it into little pieces; I pieced them together. I thought he had left the relationship. She was claiming her right to love him. He had either just received it or just retrieved it from his desk. My heart broke into more pieces than the hand-shredded letter.

If I was not losing my husband when he was having an affair, I was almost losing him in two serious car accidents. (Actually, I guess I really lost him some time before, when he told me about his intentions to cheat on me.) "Mum," as we called my mother-in-law, said after his first car accident, "This is the kind of difficult time that makes your relationship stronger." For me, it was all awful: car accidents and hurtful affairs.

When I went to thank the neurosurgeon for helping my husband after his first car accident, he replied, "I don't know why your husband isn't dead. He should be dead, but since he isn't dead, he should be paralyzed from the neck down. I didn't do anything." The paramedics had to cut his t-shirt off after the accident and later gave it to me. When I got home late that night, I took the t-shirt and held it close to me as I lay down to sleep on the couch. The t-shirt smelled like my husband. I held it closer to my face. I didn't want to sleep in the bed without him there. I shared with him and others that I knew something was going to happen before each of the accidents occurred. It was a disconcerting and disturbing awareness.

(My still-wounded heart was slashed again when, at the time of our divorce years later while my husband was continuing his most recent affair with one of his office assistants, Rita called my home and asked for him. All those years I had thought he had kept a promise not to see or talk with Rita again. Why? Why would he have Rita call? I didn't understand why he had to deliberately cause more injury. What did he gain? When I asked him about it, he didn't say anything. I continued to assume he had told her to call. Hearing my stories, Beth sensed that Rita had called on her own. She just couldn't let go.)

We bought a home in a neighboring community. Maybe my husband was having an affair at this time, too; I was not aware of it, anyway. We had fun trying to get pregnant again. And of course, it had been fun "making" the first two Knuckleheads. When John was born, my husband was in the delivery room. When he saw our son for the first time, a tear raced down his cheek. I smiled and was happy in the moment. That is the confusing irony of it all. My husband and I never stopped making love. We enjoyed each other. We had fun. We were loving toward each other.

A few years after the birth of my son, my husband's newest mistress —the last I know of—called our home one evening; I answered. "Bob is my husband, and I love him more than anything in the world. What is happening here is wrong."

She answered, "Well, who's to say?"

Forty years after my silent and suppressed aloneness began and twenty-seven years after my divorce, my dating experiences resurrected these old memories I had hidden underground. And so, here was the beginning of my downward passage into the raw woundedness of my past.

2
"I FEEL SO ALONE"

AN ASTONISHING SILENCE

All five of us were in the boat up North: Mom and Dad, my brother, my sister, and I. We were fishing for bluegills. We could hear the waves sloshing against the small boat. A stringer of fish hung off the side, the anchor off the bow. I reeled in a baby bluegill. Pulling in a fish was always exciting for everyone in the boat. "Mary's got one!"

I swung my fishing rod over to Dad and let the fish plop on the boat's wooden bottom. Dad took it off the hook and said, "Aw, Bug. This little guy is kind of small. What do you say we put him back and give him a chance to grow a bit?"

"Okay, Dad!" I said and felt relieved. I leaned over the side of the boat and rested my chin on my slightly sun-faded, red life jacket. Dad packaged the fish within his hands and held it in the water until its gills moved rhythmically again. Then he released it. My Dad is gentle and smart. I continued to rest my chin on my pillow-like lifejacket and quietly, silently thought happily about what had just happened. I listened to the sloshing water and enjoyed the gentle rocking of the boat. It was a happy and peaceful silence. In my early adulthood, my silence was of a different kind. As Dr. Beth described it as she listened to my story, "It was an astonishing silence."

My husband and I didn't have much money while he was an undergrad or later in grad school and beyond. We both worked. I worked six days a week as a waitress in a pancake house and later as I dental assistant. I used to think that if I wore some prettier clothes and cuter shoes, my husband wouldn't be cheating on me. One day I bought a soft, light blue silky top. It was short sleeved and had light pink flowers with a bit of white on it. I thought I looked pretty in it. I put it on to show my husband when he got home from school and work. When he opened the door and entered the apartment I said, "I got a new blouse today. Do you like it?"

"We should get one for Rita."

He bought the pretty blouse for his mistress; hers was pink with pale blue flowers. She came over to our house and went into our bathroom to try it on. My husband tapped the door and opened it to see her standing there. He had to know if it fit. I was standing behind him in the hallway that ran through our small apartment.

I didn't say anything.

I retreated. I backed away as far as I could down that short hallway. I wanted to hide. I didn't mean anything to him. I was alone.

It was all emblematic of an astonishing silence, a paralyzed response evidenced pre-marriage and then over and over as I continued to say nothing while he violated all decency. It was almost as if he were baiting me to speak while knowing that I wouldn't.

I had never shared this story with anyone until I shared it with my psychologist when I was fifty-nine, more than thirty years after it had happened. As I disclosed this piece of my past, I felt bad and sad. It was a sick and lonely yuckiness of moldy shame buried long ago. My psychologist said, "He wanted to see Rita in it." I needed to hear her verbalize that simple, ugly truth so I could move from denial to acceptance, so I could name the pain and heal. I couldn't identify what I was feeling then, but now I am beginning to. I was feeling shame. I was embarrassed. I had forfeited my sense of self, my personhood, my values and dreams, and had laid them all to waste in a crypt of degradation and humiliation sealed with denial. It was a pit of sadness and shameful silence layered with worthlessness and hopelessness, now at long last uncovered.

I remembered an earlier time when I locked away my feelings of desperate and lonely sadness. I was pregnant. It was before the lovely styles of clothing that reveal and celebrate the beauty of maternity, I was wearing some navy blue maternity pants with the comfortable stretchy panel. I had about three maternity shirts I thought I looked kind of okay in. That night I remember I was wearing a silky, long-sleeved slipover top that was colorful with small splashes of deep blue, red, and white. It had a collar and tied in the back. It was apparent that I was carrying a little sweetie cookie. My husband and I went out to a place to dance. His girlfriend at the time was there. I know; it is sickening.

He danced with us both. He danced with her. When the song "(You're) Having My Baby" by Paul Anka came on ("What a lovely way of saying how much you love me..."), he walked me out to the dance floor. I didn't want to dance with him then. I felt that he was just showcasing me for all to see so they would "ooh and ah" at him and think, "How sweet." They didn't know. No one knew what was really going on. I wanted to be held. I wanted to be loved and valued, but this was demeaning and sad and hurtful for me. This happened to me and to the child I carried.

Bob was still an undergrad then. When he was in graduate school, one of his grad school friends said to me, "I want you to know that I do not approve of what Bob is doing." I was silent, and I was very sad; but I did not know how to respond. I just looked at him. I did not recall the occasion, but often I reflected on his comment. Someone knew. Someone understood in some way, and that was comforting.

After the first time I shared some of my story with Beth, I felt a newfound freedom. As I left the clinic, I felt my heart lift. I had shared so much of what I had kept inside all these years. Session after session and all the days in between, God was bringing back these memories preserved in the crevasse of my silence in amazing, significant detail and vivid color.

WHY THIS EXTRA-EXTRAORDINARY SILENCE?

Sometimes it is so very difficult to record these stories from my past. My memories of them all are so acute and likewise are the attendant emotions. To see these accounts written out, to see them in black and white on my computer screen, to grasp the depth and breadth of my husband's betrayal and the extent of my desperate denial, is gravely sad and sobering. The silence was more than extraordinary; it was extra-extraordinary. Why the silence—and for so many years?

After Beth and I had been meeting for about a month, at the beginning of one session I shared with her that I had felt sad during the previous week. A very beautiful young woman who worked in the same office I worked in was expecting her second child. The whole office was excited for her and her husband. Her husband popped into the office one day; his caring and tenderness toward her were very evident and so sweet to see. At other occasions—for instance, at gatherings in the communities of friends and family—I witnessed other young husbands warmly and lovingly embracing their young and pregnant wives. I was very happy to see that and I was happy for the young women. I don't remember that ever being a scene from the drama of my marriage.

Beth listened and then said, "You are the fifty-eight-year-old Mary looking back at a young, teenage Mary." She asked me to imagine a place where Older Mary could meet with Young Mary. I picked Long Lake in the Northern Kettle Moraine, where I had often gone off-road biking. It was the kind of place both Marys would like to be.

I closed my eyes. The older Mary asked the nineteen-year-old what it was like to be her. Young Mary was quiet for some time. "I feel so alone." She paused as she sat on the picnic table bench and looked out over the lake. "I feel abandoned. Just me and the baby. I feel that I am not pretty." I started to cry.

Later, Beth played the role of Older Mary while I played Young Mary. She told me, "There is nothing you did wrong. Do not be ashamed. There is no shame here. And do not blame yourself. Your husband is the one who was broken, even before you were married. You don't have to wait for anyone to love you anymore."

Later, I was both Marys again, and I was to look Young Mary in the eyes and hug her.

I often thought that if I did more and more for my husband and if I were prettier, he could really love me then. If I drank more coffee and didn't feel so tired, he would maybe love me more. Maybe if my hair style were prettier I would be enough for him. Beth explained to me that my husband was the one broken on the inside and that my only error was not confronting him, saying "It's wrong," and leaving him.

PERSONAL WIRING

Dad tells a story about me when I was a baby. I could sit up by myself, but I wasn't walking. We still have the picture he took of me when I was sitting on the ground and holding a single blade of grass in my right hand. I was stretching my right arm high to show it to everyone. You can tell by my face I thought that blade of grass was amazing indeed. Dad said I was so happy about a simple blade of grass. My point is: I was so very happy. It was fun and safe and a happy thing to grow up in my home. So why? Why my astonishing silence?

Mom told me a story about when I was just learning how to talk. We were all sitting at the dining room table—Mom, Dad, my brother and sister, and I. Mom or Dad said something to me and I said, "No talk-a-me." I was staring at my glass of milk. "You were so little, so young. You just sat there staring at the glass and concentrating so very hard on some deep thought. We would have given anything to know what you were thinking."

I was never bored. I was always thinking, considering, pondering. My mind was never quiet. I remember that. All these thoughts and feelings I just juggled, mingled, studied, and kept to myself. Beth explained that I was programmed for passivity. It did seem to be how I was wired. In middle adulthood, I remember one of my company's vice presidents saying, "Your passivity drives me crazy." Another said, "You always know the right thing to do and say, but sometimes you hold back." He also said, "You're always so tough on yourself and beat yourself up before I even say anything."

Once, when I was walking home from grade school with some good friends, they were cutting down one of our teachers. I was upset about it. I liked her. The teachers all were different and that was simply how she was. I sort of defended her, as I recall. When they joked back, I turned to go on by myself and hollered, "Well, maybe my love is just different from yours!"

I don't know why I stormed away. I didn't know what these feelings were and had no clue how to express them. I could see that my friends just stood there for a moment, perhaps wondering what had just happened. I was wondering the same thing.

When I was in junior high, one night I was out at a restaurant with some friends. They were being goofy and were considering trying to snag some ashtrays. (This was when every table in a restaurant had at least one ashtray on it. Wow, that *was* a long time ago.) My friends could see I was getting upset and uncomfortable. "Well, it's wrong. It's just wrong." Once again, I didn't understand what I was feeling, so I wanted to leave.

"Mary, we'll put them back. We won't take them. It's all cool."

Another time, I responded to something and my mom and brother said, "You old, stubborn German!" I cried a little and ran down the stairs. I didn't know what being "a stubborn German" meant, but I guess I thought it was something terrible. "Mary, we're just kidding. We're just being funny." They never called me that again. (Funny thing is, when I thought about it years later, I would laugh. Because if anyone is stubborn and German, it would be me.)

As I described my past, Beth keenly pointed out, "No one ever told you that you had rights." That was a wake-up statement for me and indeed, the question of rights has played a big part in the whole dynamic of my life. She also identified my childhood as a "Beaver Cleaver childhood" in which conflict and learning how to identify and express feelings were avoided. My ignorance of a claim to rights, the evasion of conflict, a lack of awareness of feelings and inexperience in identifying and expressing them—along with my passive temperament—created a fertile soil for invasive emotional abuse to take over and destroy the garden. The only viable plant seemed to be a paralyzed, frozen silence.

Beth perceived that I was easily shamed. The shame and the denial that the relationship was over, hanging on and hoping for things to change, and always protecting (even defending) Bob contributed greatly to my silence. She sensed in me a fear of being transparent and vulnerable. My temperament, my computer chip, my DNA, my personality imprint for passivity and my intricate internal wiring to keep feelings to myself all worked together to secure my silence and suppress my emotions and my stories.

"I give you permission to no longer protect Bob. You don't have to protect him anymore." Hearing that was like unlocking handcuffs I had latched on. I was now able to venture down this deep crevasse using both hands. Beth shared with me that I often put my hand over my mouth as I spoke: a nonverbal expression of shame. It is refreshing to realize that as we continued on this journey, I did this less and less. Beth's permission to let go of shame enabled me to put my headlamp on the brightest setting to direct the light into the darkness of the vast crevasse and see more clearly.

BURIED SADNESS

Listening to my stories, Beth commented that I had received confusing messages: *He loves me, he loves me not.* They were emotionally baffling. Beth described Bob as a polygamist. She stated that I am strong, a very strong woman. I don't have anything to prove. God loves me. I can be transparent and vulnerable. "You buried sadness." Beth added that it could be very important to let my children know of the sadness I had buried.

I had mentioned in one of our first sessions that when I was nineteen and pregnant, I had been so concerned that my deep sadness would affect my sweet Honey Cake while she was inside of me. Beth agreed that my children would have known the sadness when they were inside of me and in the home environment.

When I first shared part of my story with my Joy, I didn't realize that I had actually still held something back to protect her from knowledge and alarm until the insight from Dr. Beth. It was not just the fact that her father hadn't attended the birthing classes. I did not reveal the extramarital relationship my husband had while I was pregnant with her. I had failed to protect her then. Something bad happened to us, and in that sense I had failed to protect my daughter from it. "It is difficult to face and take the responsibility for having affected someone else's future." I had failed to protect her by not challenging the situation I was in then. I have no excuse. I am sorry. (If I ever write another book, it can't possibly be more difficult than this one.)

I did tell Joy how I had prayed for her while I carried her inside of me. I prayed that the deep sadness I held in would not affect her. I asked God to take care of her and not let it hurt her. I was only nineteen and read as many books and magazines on pregnancy and parenting as I could get my hands on. I ate well; I took my neonatal vitamins. However, I didn't know the "prescription" to alter my situation. I did not rescue Joy and protect her from the sadness being inflicted on her. In the same passivity of not challenging my situation, I did not challenge hers. Typing this out, however many times, has made all this clearer.

———————————

We must not fail to challenge injustice when we see it.

———————————

Along with the fear of vulnerability and of being known, pride is also a big factor that encourages silence. Disclosure makes you real and helps others see you as human. I remember always feeling that I was not good enough—less than others. I wonder if that is a warped pride. Yes, I daresay it is.

As I described those years of my marriage and my relationship with my husband, Beth clarified how I had forfeited myself and made Bob an idol in my life. In *I Quit!: Stop Pretending Everything Is Fine and Change Your Life*, Geri Scazzero writes, "Fusion is a term from physics that describes what happens when metals are melted together and lose their distinctive qualities. Emotional fusion happens when we lose our distinctiveness and lose ourselves in someone else's life." (p. 203) I had lost myself in my husband's life. I lived for him.

I have intuitive, prophetic capacities, but also a reluctance to insert myself into a situation. I fail to insert my will or my preferences. I fail to insert myself and thus fail to influence a situation. Along with passivity programming and being overly worried, a paralysis then sets in. Paralyzed, frozen, uninvolved. Beth noted that I am fearful of making the wrong move. It's a terrible feeling, being frozen—waiting for someone else to act, perhaps. Then there is the huge factor of denial.

———————————

You can clearly influence a situation. Your gift allows you to know how.

———————————

My father said to me on two different occasions: "Mary, a mind is a terrible thing to waste." And now, I would add, "If you have a gift for intuitive knowing, awareness, and discernment, failure to act is..." But I have been struggling to find the right word for some time now—even as I retyped that thought. Mine is the greater sin, the greater failure: a failure to act.

After a session with Beth in April 2011, I sat by the lake outside the Lakefront Wellness Center and prayed: *Lord, I give you all this learning. Change me. Lord, let me; help me to be the Mary you want me to be. Forgive me for not inserting myself into situations where I could influence for good. Holy Spirit, you have gifted me in so many ways. Help me, work through me to employ these gifts with courage, certainty, clarity, faith, and truth for your sake and for your Kingdom. Father, Son and Holy Spirit chase out the junk and false self; fill me with yourself. Let the battle begin.*

I used to question my lovability if anyone were to know what I did. I recall how, whenever I was injured or emotionally hurt, I would retreat and deal with it in privacy. A few years ago, I had the wonderful opportunity to reconnect with a high school friend. It's a fun story and a grand discovery of renewed friendship. I had already shared part of my story with her, but now I wanted to share one of my most difficult admissions. I cried as I asked her, "If I tell you this part, will you still love me?"

She immediately stood up, as I then did as well. "Of course I will," she assured me as she cried and gave me a big hug.

Priceless pearls of wisdom from Beth that I should wear as a bracelet next to my watch to remind me whenever I check the time: "It's okay to influence the world around you, and God really wants you to know that you can. It is a matter of extreme importance that you get involved." And "You don't need to reprogram all of your personal programming. There are positive aspects to it all: You are responsible, predictable, and solid. You are a safe place for people and you are dependable. You are open to all people and truly care about all people. You love and value them."

Beth encouraged me to write an impact statement to Bob as if he would read it. "This is how your actions affected me. Stand up for yourself! Defend yourself! Go back in time and say what you did not say!" When I disclosed that Bob had said to me that he did not have to say he was sorry, Beth awakened me to the realization that he was being arrogant and that I had allowed him to belittle me once again. (As I type this, a startling notion popped into my mind: Maybe he isn't sorry.)

I had picked up Henri Nouwen's *The Inner Voice of Love: A Journey Through Anguish to Freedom* at Beth's recommendation, and I previewed the table of contents as I sat in the waiting room. I anticipated an interesting book. One chapter that jumped out at me was: "Let Your Lion Lie Down with Your Lamb." I turned to page 78 and read, "The art of spiritual living is to fully claim both your lion and your lamb. Then you can act assertively without denying your own needs. And you can ask for affection and care without betraying your talent to offer leadership." It's clear that I was drawn to it and had the opportunity to read it before my appointment. *Thank you, God. This was the perfect piece to read and ponder.*

It felt good to know that Beth listened to my story and heard my feelings as I shared things, session after session. I recalled recently sharing a current situation with another good friend. When people reacted, it was like *Wow, they feel that, too*—their responses matched mine.

In my journal I would convert Beth's "you" statements about me to "I" statements, so I could accept immediate ownership of what I was learning about myself. Examples of such converted and valuable statements include:

I rendered myself insignificant by holding back and not daring to confront. Passivity can be born of fear and restraint. And it is a part of my temperament. My holding back because of this fear and restraint makes my contribution less significant. I need to insert myself; I have much to offer. I am protective of myself. I have a desire to avoid any cost to myself. Ironically, there is a cost to no action to others and to myself.

I also can create a need for myself.

I have the gift of prophecy.

I am passive and restrained with my gifts of discernment, wisdom, and prophecy. According to the Bible, it is "wicked" to put "talent" in the sand and to bury wisdom and gifts in the sand. Failure, restraint, or refusal to insert myself is a critical missed opportunity to serve in the moment. Responding in this way, I miss the full opportunity of my calling.

I have sensed it, too. I restrain myself, hold back, and don't confront. I see others who do, but I can't. Beth pointed out, "Holding back and reluctance to confront can also prevent you from encouraging people." I responded that encouragement is a gift I have and use regularly. Encouraging people in all areas of my life gives me great joy. I thrive on it. I *desire* to do it. I suppose it is far less risky and does not carry such a great threat of being wrong, so I don't hold back on encouraging others. Beth added that the more I trust and act on intuition and gifts, and also hear with the Holy Spirit's ears, the more capable I will become in employing the gift of prophecy.

"Pray!" she said, "for the Holy Spirit to be your co-counselor, co-chaplain." I need the Lord by my side and the Holy Spirit whispering in my ear. I pray for a yielded heart and for the Father's love and strength and courage. I pray for the courage of Jesus.

"You are performing at the helm. You need the Holy Spirit sitting next to you as a co-therapist. Ask him to allow you to hear what he hears, to comprehend what is really going on."

Help me to hear. Help me to be willing, totally willing to help. Help me to listen and trust your gifting and guidance.

Dr. Beth advised that I should consider someone I could share "being known" with besides her. "Pray to the Holy Spirit for this. Ask him to show you who you should share your story with."

3
TELLING THE STORY AND
BREAKING THE SILENCE

I had prayed through my session notes. It was a powerful exercise. I prayed about my place at the helm, inserting myself, and sharing my story. After praying, I found myself empowered to put the learning into practice.

At one of my worksites a young man on break asked me, "Okay, so, answer this question for me. Is it fair that someone who says yes to God at the very end of his life gets to go to heaven when someone else has lived it their whole life? How can that be fair?" I was soliciting the Holy Spirit's input when another person in the room said, "Well, you know, Mary wasn't always a chaplain."

At that, he waved his hand and headed back to his workstation. I finished my visit and started the drive home, but I had an answer to his question. I thought: *Well, maybe next week I will have a chance to get into a conversation with him. If I head back now, he will be working and busy and I won't be able to talk with him anyway.*

Mary, insert yourself! Turn the car around and get back to the loading dock! Maybe he will be there, maybe not. Try! I made a U-turn and went back to the warehouse. Jack was driving the forklift. "Jack! I have an answer to your question. I was on the way home and got a directive to come back here and find you.

You are important. And when God is giving the order, it is best that I just turn the car around and get back here."

He paused, leaned back against the lift, and folded his arms. "Okay. Let's hear it." He smiled.

"Well, first of all, here's the thing. When I was least lovable, someone told me I mattered to God. I asked him into my life and nothing has been the same since. I was thirty-seven. So, for the past twenty-plus years, I have been a Christian. And I think you are right. It is not fair. It is not fair that I have known the love and friendship and support of an incredible God for all these years. My life is so much better with him in it. I have hope. And when someone who is at his death bed at last asks God into his life, no, it is not fair that he lived so long on this earth not knowing God as his father. It is not fair that I was able to know God as my father for so many years."

Jack unfolded his arms and leaned forward. He smiled. "That was a good answer." As he turned back to the controls on the forklift he said, "Thanks for coming back and finding me. See you next week."

Later that week, I had a conversation with Mom and Dad in the den. They were sitting next to each other on the couch while I was sitting on a chair kitty-corner from them. I started to share my story. Mom leaned in closer. Dad moved closer to her and leaned in. They were both hanging onto every word I said. "We didn't know. Mary, we didn't know. Thanks for confiding in us now." And later as I headed upstairs, Dad called from the den to say again, "Thanks for confiding in us, Mary."

I cried as I finished sharing this encounter with Beth. It was a sudden, loud, and abrupt cry. Beth leaned forward and said, "Please give your parents a big hug for me." She added, "Family systems affect how we respond to things." She described how mine was and is a cooperating system: one with avoidance. Any change changes the whole system. And there is a cost to no action.

Once I got going, I kept on telling my story. I shared part of it with my brother. He said, "You never said anything when you were going through the divorce, and you acted as if everything was okay. We thought, 'Wow! Superhuman!'" I felt relief as I shared my story with my brother, my lifelong friend.

In another telling with my friend Barbara, I let my sadness and aloneness in my marriage be known. As I began to disclose a piece of my story, I learned that she, too, had never shared her story with anyone. She had been married for twenty-five years, enduring experiences not unlike my own. Is it not sadly amazing how we both had accused ourselves? *If I were pretty enough, assertive enough, strong enough, didn't have varicose veins, had prettier clothes and prettier shoes, this wouldn't be happening.* In both stories, husbands (now ex-husbands) never acknowledged they had hurt us. Each telling of my story reinforced my need to be heard and my need to hear the stories of others.

I was out for dinner with my new friend Nancy. She was listening to my story as I told it between bites of salad. At one point, she sighed and said, "Give this woman a drink!" When our plates of fish arrived, she coached, "You need to forgive yourself." As we were taking the last bites of our potato pancakes, she added, "Your husband wanted to bring you into his addiction." She listened to my story for a long time; I listened to hers. Her friendship and concerned listening to my story were just what I needed.

Being known is essential. Being real and sharing my story, revealing sadness and shame, and disclosing my brokenness in safety were imperative for recovery to take place.

I shared my story with Jenny as we sipped coffee and munched on bagels. As she listened, her nonverbal response was affirming and validating. She was sad to hear my deep sadness. It was very dear. Right after my disclosure, she let herself be known in regard to a challenging situation with one of her parents. Self-disclosure invites others to share their own stories.

During this month of becoming known, I shared part of my story with Ginny. She is a good friend, a very wise friend. I hesitated and said, "This part is difficult." I told her that when my husband was going to Lake Venience with one of his employees, he said I should get together with the employee's husband. They also were friends of ours. And I did. The guilt was so huge for me. In time, I was the one who moved out to live in an apartment.

Ginny said, "And he is the one who should have been leaving."

I told her how Mum, my former mother-in-law, told me, "Mary, you have to let it go. You have beaten yourself up enough." Another close female relative said, "Well, it's about time."

As I shared my story with Ginny, I added, "I want to make sure I go through it all. I want to be done."

She responded, "You are never really done."

4
HEARTBREAKING RECALL, RAGE UNLEASHED, RELEASE EXTENDED

ANOTHER HEARTBREAK MOMENT

After this particular day of sharing, I recalled another heartbreak moment. My husband had told me about a letter from Leslie, a friend of ours. Bob had introduced Leslie and her husband, Rich, to me. We were living in our third home, the one we were living in when I found the love letter from Rita, whom he said he wanted to have a child with. Bob read Leslie's letter to me. I have blocked out the details. It was awful. It referred to an affair Bob was having with her. Bob told me about the letter, read it to me, and then said it didn't happen. I didn't even know my husband had gotten a letter from Leslie. Why did he bring it up? To hurt me more? To maintain control of me? I wonder if he just wanted to see my reaction. I couldn't take any more. It seems now that he must have lied when he said nothing had happened.

Or was his disclosure a preemptive measure in the event Leslie intended (and perhaps had threatened) to make the truth known? I had not pondered this possibility before. Yet it fits with the pattern of the way his other lovers acted.

Did Bob ever really love me? I had been deceived and now was slowly awakening to my entrenched state of denial. He probably did have an affair with Leslie. It all made sense as the pieces fell together.

My husband had invited Leslie and Rich over to our home. We finished dinner and were sitting in the living room. The three of them had been talking in sign language; Leslie and Rich were both hearing impaired. I was not very adept at the language. I picked up on some things, but essentially, I was just watching them. I got up to go into the kitchen. Rich got up and seemed to be motioning for me to go into the bedroom. I thought he was just joking around and I felt quite awkward. Then he took my arm and continued trying to persuade me to go into the bedroom. Bob just sat there on the sofa. I was embarrassed. I tried to believe he was just joking around, and I didn't like it. I looked toward Bob for help. He had moved closer to Leslie. I had said no, no to Rich and continued on my way to the kitchen.

At some point in this particular session of sharing with Beth, I used the phrase "dating this couple" without thinking, referring to Rich and Leslie.

Beth said, "Well, that was an interesting Freudian slip."

"What?" I asked.

"You said, *dating this couple.*"

Where the heck did that come from? As I was forced to look back and see the puzzle pieces, I now understood that is what my husband was setting up. (Again I have stopped typing. I am groaning as I bury my forehead in my hands.)

RAGE

I had written the following in my journal. Perhaps this fits my "homework assignment" from Beth to write an impact statement to Bob as if he would read it:

How could Bob, and why would he want this to happen to me? Sadness and shame, disgust and disgrace hit me and sent me sliding dangerously down the crevasse. *Damn you, Bob! What a fucking jerk you were. How dare you dishonor me so? Your wife! The mother of your children! Mary! Me! (I thought of my husband with all those different women.) You used me! You lied to me! You betrayed me! You shamed me! You dishonored me! You were disloyal. You did not love and cherish me. You did not honor me. You in no way and by no means respected me.*

I agree with the assessment that you were a polygamist and a parasite. I did everything for you. I gave up my dreams to help you and support you in pursuing yours. I lost myself. I gave up my goals, my person, and in the end my very values. I gave up my fidelity at the end of our marriage. That was what you wanted. In any regard, I did then and now certainly take responsibility for my sin. I knew and acknowledged my guilt and my moral shame. In my passivity I forfeited myself. I lost my self. I forgot how to feel. I gave up my person. I betrayed myself and I betrayed God. I made you an idol and greatly sinned against God. God forgive me. You were a fucking bastard. A liar. A cheat. A scoundrel. A jerk. An ass. A betrayer. A selfish, arrogant shit. You treated me so disgustingly. You didn't love me. I stood by you and loved you unconditionally. I lived a life of denial, believing that you loved me. Yes, except for the fact that God created our three children and all that comes with and about that, I wish I had never met you, never knew you, and it would be just fine with me if I never saw you again. I never told anyone about how you treated me. I kept it to myself all these forty years. I protected you. I protected our children. You told others that we were getting a divorce because of my affair. You arrogant ass.

You never told me you were sorry. In those dark years after our divorce when you never ever said you were sorry yet claimed a newfound faith, you set up and maintained a wall, a barricade to my capacity to believe there is a God.

Years later when I spoke with you and you still refused to say you were sorry, my feelings were reinvalidated. My pain disregarded and reinflicted. Fueled by your selfish pride, you stepped on me then, and now again. I was devoted to you, loved and cared for you, stood by you, supported you, protected your reputation and your name. When you said you would not say you were sorry, you slapped me in the face. You slammed me in the stomach. Before, I saw no way out. Before, I was alone. Before, I felt worthless. Things are different now.

In Jesus's name and having been forgiven and redeemed, I release forgiveness to Bob. You limit your potential if you turn from the convicting of the Holy Spirit and continue to refuse to surrender your pride and confess to me and to our children the full disclosure of agony you caused. In the very recent past, you still have refused to do so.

GOING DEEPER

I thought I had forgiven Bob a long time ago. And yes, I had, in fact. But now I was going deeper into the pain, anguish, and injury I had denied and suppressed for so very long. This now was a present release of rage, a necessary step in the journey of the downward climb. This, I believe, is the place where we dread to tread, a place where we realize and acknowledge the deepest trauma that then demands a new level and awareness of forgiveness. Forgiveness had to go deeper into the crevasse.

Confession is a necessary step if forgiveness is to be received. Theologians Green and Lawrenz explain that confession is required in order for us to reconnect with our God. Likewise, confession makes reconnection possible between the offended and the offender. In *Encountering Shame and Guilt*, Green and Lawrenz clarify that "Forgiveness is recognizing the wrong, holding the person who transgressed responsible for that wrong, and, in the light of this, choosing not to punish. Forgiveness is the application of grace and truth. Truth is evidenced by the attribution of responsibility to the wrongdoer; grace is offered through the extension of the gift of love and release." (pp. 59–60)

I once emailed to Bob: "You are a child of God, and you are in His heart, hands and care and you will be in His heaven. That is where I leave you, in the hands of God."

What happened? Why? Why did I give in? Give up? Deny myself?
Live for someone else? Give up my dreams? Deny my feelings?
I made him an idol. God forgive me!

A New Conversation with Myself

Here, then, is a testimony to how far I have come in the years of growth since leaving my husband and the invisible identity he required of me, and compelled me to comply with. This is what I will tell myself: *I am pretty. I am smart and wise. I am intelligent and discerning. I am an athlete. I am a theologian. I am a scholar. I am a mother. I am a grandmother. I am a friend. I am an ambassador. I am a friend to people around the world. I am strong. I am good. I am a preacher. I am a missionary. I am a trainer. I am a teacher. I am a chaplain. I am a leader. I am a biker. I am a runner. I am a swimmer. I am a triathlete. I am a mountain climber. I am a strength trainer. I am a feminist. I am an off-road biker. I am a track bike racer. I am a supervisor. I am an executive. I am a sister. I am a sales specialist. I am a dental assistant. I am a coach. I am an amazing human being. I am a child of God. I have the gift of prophecy. I have the gift of encouragement. I have the gift of preaching and teaching. I am a writer. I have the gift of God's wisdom. I have the gift of discernment. I am a world traveler. I am an activist. I am a disciple of Jesus Christ. I am an evangelist. I have varicose veins and wrinkles and I am pretty. I am an exceptionally strong woman. I am charming and witty. And I am loved.*

5
BREAKAWAY: RIDE MY BIKE
AND RIDE IT HARD

Biking is my favorite sport. It has been for a long time—for as long as I can remember. I like to ride bikes with brakes and without brakes. I like to ride on old rails, trails, tracks, and roads. I recall that when I was pregnant with my son, I told myself that I was going to exercise during the pregnancy. I wanted to be as healthy and strong as I could be for the pregnancy and the delivery. Although I loved biking best, I thought that swimming would be safer to pursue throughout my pregnancy. Swimming would help the poor circulation I had in my legs. I started swimming laps at the YMCA, and pretty soon I was swimming a mile. As the months went on and the baby grew, I felt more and more like a penguin bobbing in the water. My son was born in July 1980.

Gary, a good friend of ours, said, "You know, you just have to add running and you could do a triathlon." That was in March of 1981. I started running. I did my first triathlon three months later in June. It was a half-mile swim, a twenty-five-mile bike ride, and a 10k run.

I was feeling good about my body. I felt strong. I had shared with Beth how my husband was not supportive of me doing the Second Annual Menomonie Tinman Triathlon in September of that same year. It would be a one-mile swim in the cold waters of Lake Menomin in Menomonie, Wisconsin, followed by a fifty-five-mile bike ride including the famed and brutal Turkey Hill, and a thirteen-mile run. Bob discouraged my training, so I trained like a weekend warrior. With what little time I had, I was relentless. I was feeling better and better about myself. It was one of the rare times I did something for myself in ten years.

My husband had taken flying lessons and eventually owned a plane. Early in our marriage it was go-karting and watching car races. Anyway, he wanted to fly the two of us and my bike to the Tinman Tri. Before the race, he was absorbed in talking about flying us back home and his concern for the weather. He continued this message as he rode alongside me in part of the run. It was hot—eighty-plus degrees with a cloudless blue sky. In the last leg of this race, the only things that didn't hurt were my eyelashes; and I wasn't too sure about them. As I was trying to push myself through the very last stretch of the race with a determination to finish, my husband was acting as if I should bail out so we could get in the plane and head home. I amazed myself in how I refused to quit.

Then, as I kicked it out to the finish line, he shouted out, "Let's give the little lady a hand." I was alone in training for this. He had discouraged me all the way. When I had needed his encouragement, it was not there. He was not there for me and now he pulls this? He did not earn the right to cross this finish line with me. He had waived it a long time ago. I saw it as just another time he did not have my interests at heart. This was my race. This was my win. I did it for me. This was my victory. A mile swim in a cold, spring-fed lake, a fifty-five-mile bike ride with Turkey Hill in it—only one killer among many others—and a thirteen-mile run.

The Tinman and Biking Hard, September 6, 1981

I crossed the finish line. One guy handed me a fantastic medal and another man handed me an ice-cold beer. "That's what I need," I said.

The man who gave me the beer laughed and said, "I know, I know. You're a cheap drunk. Congratulations, you did it!" I smiled a huge smile and laughed. Yes, I did it. I had a feeling of freedom, a feeling I only knew when I rode my bike and rode it hard.

This finish line that demanded all I could be and all I could give was the catalyst for the revival of Mary.

It took me six hours, thirty-two minutes, and ten seconds. Not too shabby for a mother of three who had just started training six months before. I was just delighted to cross the finish line. Triathlons were a new thing at the time. Not many women participated then, actually. There were 198 finishers out of 210 athletes who participated. I placed 156th overall: 154th in the swim, 153rd in the bike, and 147th in the run. As we were waiting for the race to start, I overheard one guy say, "I can't believe how many women are here," and he looked over at me. As I was coming in on my run, I looked across the road to notice him heading out on his run. He recognized me as well and shook his head in disbelief that I was actually ahead of him in the race.

Quick detour, from past to present: I told Beth how I had gone to a wine bar that week and had a glass of wine with a yummy appetizer. While I was there, the fellow I had just started to date through the dating service called my cell to see what I was up to and said he would like to join me. So we had a glass of wine together. Eventually in our conversation, I asked him if he had been faithful to his wife, who had died about a year earlier. He said no.

"It's over!" I said.

He responded, "I told you the truth."

"I have to leave." I picked up my things and walked out.

I told Beth I couldn't believe I did that! I was so dramatic. Good grief! I laughed at myself. I had only known the man for about two weeks. We had had a bagel and coffee one day and went to a movie another time. I didn't know how I would ever show up at the wine bar again. Thank goodness only two other people were there, along with the owner. (A side note: the Friday night Raul and I went to the movie, I saw the man I had been engaged to about six years after my divorce. What is the likelihood of that? I recognized him as he was running through the mall to the movie theatre and then as he stood in line for tickets. I hadn't seen him for twenty-two years. What a week of drama.)

Beth coached, "You transferred your emotions toward Bob onto Raul. You were walking out on Bob. This was actually a very positive step."

For the record, I called Raul and apologized. He actually was all okay with the whole thing. He was generous in his understanding.

A DISTURBING ACQUIESCENCE

It seems to me that I had wanted to get my PhD ever since I was in kindergarten. I loved school. When a new school year started, I couldn't wait to get the new books. I loved how they smelled and I couldn't wait to learn what was inside. I studied hard and enjoyed it. I excelled academically. The traditional classroom learning methods worked well for me. I earned an academic scholarship for the college I wanted to attend in Illinois. But after meeting Bob, I began to release that dream and eventually let it go in order to support my husband as he pursued his dreams.

When I was a kid in second grade, I couldn't wait until third grade, when I would get to learn German. In third grade, my brother had started learning German; my sister, Russian. The summer before I started third grade, I was told that now we wouldn't be learning a foreign language until sixth grade. So, that summer, I found my brother's German language instruction papers and started to teach myself German. I learned the alphabet, counting, and a number of words.

I enjoyed learning the German language and enjoyed learning about Germany, its geography, its culture, and its customs. I worked hard at it because it was important to me and I loved it. Soon, one of my dreams was to go to Germany. In my junior year of high school, my German teacher invited me to go to Germany with her for the entire summer and tour the whole country. I turned down the opportunity. Bob didn't want me to go.

How did I ever get to the point of so quickly turning down something I had worked toward and longed for? And to let go of my scholarship for the college I wanted to attend to attain the degree I wanted to earn? So I wouldn't disappoint or disgruntle my jealous boyfriend, after dating him for just a number of months. I look back now and see myself forfeiting my dreams. So many things I had been striving for so many years were actually coming to fruition. They were not only within reach, but at my fingertips; not only at my fingertips, but in my grasp.

I started playing the saxophone in third grade. That was fun, too. My sister played the clarinet; my brother, the trumpet. It was crazy the way our beagle would howl when we practiced our instruments. All we had to do was raise the mouthpiece to our lips and he would start howling. It was hysterical. Jan and I took turns practicing in our small, walk-in closet. Anyway, my high school band was incredible; our director was tough and he was good. We all admired him. We called him Boss. If you were in the symphonic band, you were in the marching band, too. All band members would have the opportunity to go on a band trip in their sophomore, junior, or senior year. So every three years, the band would perform out of state. For me, it would be my senior year. Yes, I did it again. I told Boss I couldn't go. Bob was with me when I told him. I don't know how I explained it. You see, Bob didn't want me to go. He was jealous and he didn't want me to go away. Why did I relinquish control? I was just seventeen. What was going on? What was I afraid of? What was I thinking? This trip was something all of the school musicians looked forward to. We were going to DC to perform in the Cherry Blossom Parade. I was the one who let it rain on my own parade. I was the one. I was the one. I was the one. And I don't understand why.

In my senior year, I was elected to be class secretary. I was sad that I found myself spending less and less time with my friends. I was actually beginning to feel that I was maybe kind of pretty. The guys were taking a second glance. It was kind of nice. I loved high school. I had been in school with many of the other teens since we were all in kindergarten. And here we were. And here I was, doing I don't-know-what. I loved public speaking. I really enjoyed speech class. It was another class I had been looking forward to for a long time. I had wanted to be a missionary in grade school. Once, I actually preached for our youth group.

The accomplishments of my adolescent identity were surprisingly fragile. They did not hold and I gave them up little by little. You have read it. I forfeited myself. I idolized Bob. I denied my own discernment. I relinquished my dreams. In time, I chose to abandon my faith. In time, I chose to abandon my God.

As I paged through my journal, I noted the prayers I wrote and prayed as I discovered what I had done wrong. I prayed for forgiveness and God's help. Likewise, when I visited the homes where I had lived during my marriage, I was asking God to forgive me for specific sins, including forfeiting my dreams and sharing myself before marriage. I asked him to forgive me for what I still don't see and don't understand. *Thank you for Joy, Katy, and John and now the Six—plus five grandchildren. Use my learning now to shape me into what you want me to be.*

I want to be obedient to God. I will not abandon the dreams and desires he has given me. I will not let myself be suppressed or oppressed by anyone. I am valuable and have a personal role with gifts and talents and opportunities from God. I do not have anything to prove. I can be transparent. I can be vulnerable. I can be known.

My disturbing acquiescence, a troubling submission, a choking compliance—all required and resulted from a burial of emotions. I denied my feelings and shoved them over the edge of the crevasse. When I returned to college at age twenty-nine, only a few months before I reached the landmark age of thirty, I made every course bleed to help me understand and make some sense of what I had gone through and what I had experienced in marriage and what I was then experiencing in divorce and life as a single mom. Learning from early psychology courses and more advanced human development studies, in communication coursework from Human Communication 101 and Cross-Cultural Communication through advanced studies in my major, from women's studies and women's literature; I learned about emotions and the expression of feelings. I was becoming able to intellectualize around all of this madness. For so many years, I held tough emotions at bay and presented a happy and carefree Mary to the world. This collegiate journey helped me to begin to unravel the why of some of my recent past and define some of the emotions, including the acceptance of anger and comprehension of what it could mean, the role it played, and how to deal with it. There was more work to be done, but it was a beginning, and it made a difference in my life.

As I was letting go of the dream of a life with my husband who would love me and care about me, I was reaching for another dream. I was in an environment where I had known success in the past and was stepping back into the world of books and learning, speaking, and writing that I was happy in. People who knew me before my marriage would tell me, "Wow. We have Mary back again." Those who had only met me during my marriage said, "Wow. You have really changed. You are so much more alive and dynamic." Others who knew my husband from grad school said, "You always had to live in Bob's shadow. You can be Mary now." My father said to me, "I thought I would in time be visiting my daughter at South Division [a mental treatment facility]."

I began to find myself again. I let myself investigate anger and figure out how to express it. I actually let myself imagine kicking my ex-husband in the ass and sending him into orbit around Pluto. I was learning about human emotions. I wanted to learn how to recognize them. I needed to be able to detect and differentiate emotions. For a long time I had wanted to be able to understand what I was feeling and to be able to say what I wanted to say in real time, in the moment—not after the fact. I did not want to continue in the forever pattern of I should have said A or I should have done B.

In my marriage relationship, I ignored my emotions to a greater and greater degree. Ignorant of the concept of boundaries, I disowned thoughts and feelings, abandoned hopes and dreams, and eventually, values and beliefs, in exchange for those of my husband. My personal identity, just beginning to stand strong, was subverted and toppled in this relationship that was becoming less and less healthy.

From more than one college text, I learned that when I fail to take account of anger and push it underground, I instead accept a lesser image of myself. I have essentially said that I do not have rights and am of lesser value. The anger I would not look at all those years was trying to say, "This is not okay. It is wrong for you to be treated like this." It was a transforming breakthrough to identify anger, yet anger can sort of co-occur with other emotions. I suppressed other feelings as well. I didn't know I was doing that. Your well-being is affected when you bury anger. How can other feelings not be numbed by the oozing, however deep, from an unattended wound? During my undergraduate studies, I did not go deeper into sadness and shame, loneliness and fear. The downward climb would take me there.

6

GIVING UP ON GOD AND GIVING UP ON LIFE

THROWING OUT THE BABY WITH THE MANGER

It must have been 1983. I was in a place where the hurt was huge, disappointment was overwhelming, and discouragement reigned. I gave up on God. I remember saying to my now ex-husband, "Don't you think God is just a fairy tale?"

I had grown up in a churched home. I loved going to church and I loved learning about the Bible. I had wanted to be a missionary when I grew up. I was in the habit of praying before meals and before I went to bed. That changed during this passage in the journey of my life. I taught myself not to pray. If I would catch myself beginning to pray, I would stop short and say, "No. No! I won't do this. I'm not going to do this anymore."

Christmas came around that year. One night, after my three young children were asleep, I walked by our traditional old nativity set under the Christmas tree. I paused, bent down, and picked up the painted clay manger with the baby Jesus. I cupped it in my hand, looked at it, and walked to the front door. I opened the door and stepped outside onto the front cement step. As I stepped forward with my left foot, I raised my right arm, brought it back, and then launched the clay figurine as hard as I could. I threw out the baby with the manger. It landed somewhere across the street in the neighbor's yard. Jesus was just a fairy tale, and I couldn't believe the story.

READY TO THROW MY LIFE OUT

One day (it must have been shortly after the divorce in October of 1983), I picked up the city newspaper. As I began reading the front page, I realized that a reporter who had a daily front-page column had interviewed my former husband in his practice. The story would circulate all over the greater metropolitan area, including into the suburbs and the southeastern part of the state, and farther still. More people than I wanted to imagine would be reading the popular column as they sipped their morning coffee.

The news reporter had taken his notes and written the copy. He recorded the story as told by the man I loved and lived for. The writer jotted down the description my husband gave of his practice and how it had come to be. Bob spoke of his successes and all that went into them. He spoke of his pilot's license and his private airplane. My name was never mentioned; my person, not remembered. My sacrifice given, totally disregarded. I was left out, deleted, erased. The story in bold, black ink on the front page said much about my high school sweetheart. My name, purposefully omitted by Bob, revealed a story behind the story. I had loved him unconditionally. I had let go of my dreams so he could pursue his. I had worked hard. I had stood by his side even when my heart and well-being were trampled on. I had worked as a waitress six days a week and later I had worked as a dental assistant. Often, I was working both jobs. My idol made the front page, and the memory of me wouldn't even make the obituaries. I felt alone, hurt, like someone who did not matter: one who did not warrant mention.

I was already sinking in a quicksand of trauma and depression when I received a letter from the Catholic Church informing me that my marriage to my husband, the father of my children, was being annulled by the church. It was a full-page, single-spaced letter reporting this declaration in numerous statements, each one stinging more than the other, until I felt like I had received multiple stab wounds to my heart. The church where my wedding was held over a decade ago was proclaiming that my marriage never happened.

Pepper, my cat, had been missing for three days. My children were not at home with me but at their father's home, where wedding plans were probably in the making. My parents were out of town. I was alone that night trying to tackle my college homework, the trail to recovery of a dream abandoned years before. My heart's murmurings were dark; my thoughts were darker still. I called a new friend. I thought if I could hear someone's voice and hear that things were okay, I would be able to release these despairing thoughts of suicide.

This new friend could not be there for me just then. He was not able to speak with me at the time. I mumbled something like, "That's okay," said good-bye, and hung up the phone. Now I was contemplating how I could, how I would kill myself. After a lonely interlude of sitting in the dark night of my undefined emotional essence, I stood up. I walked to my living room couch and sat down. Then, I lay down. I slept for four to five minutes, no longer. The exploitive cloud moved away. I got up and did the next thing. I returned to my studies.

The next morning, I felt drained beyond any measure known to me before. I felt as if I had been run over by a truck. My neighbor came over early that morning. "I saw the paper, Mary. You must have been devastated. It must have hurt you deeply."

This was another moment in my story when someone reached out and I experienced one of the rare glimmers of realization that my hurting made sense. My neighbor had read the article and expected that I would feel like this. Someone knew. Someone understood a part of my story. I had a brief gift of company in my cavern built of emotions that as yet I couldn't name.

About a year later, I crossed paths with the friend who had not been able to speak with me when I called that dark night. He wanted to get together for lunch and coffee. We did. We each had a salad at a restaurant I don't even think is around anymore. He said, "I am so sorry."

Presuming what he might be leading into, I started to say, "It's okay," but realized that I needed to allow him to share, to express what he was feeling just then, right then.

He continued. "I am so sorry. Your voice. Your voice! I am so sorry I was not there for you. Your voice. I could have helped and I didn't. I am sorry."

I told him that I understood. He could not be there for me in that moment. I understood. "Your sharing this with me now helps a lot." I knew someone could see; someone could grasp a bit of what I was feeling. "Thank you."

One or two years after my husband's story made the news, I met an old friend who had also been a waitress at the pancake restaurant before and after I was married. We ran into each other at a swim meet that both of our kids were competing in. I had not seen her for ten years or so. The very first thing she said to me was, "Mary, when I read that story in the newspaper, I was so sad. All the customers…you remember our morning regulars that had a baby shower for you? Well, they all said, 'Where's Mary? Why isn't Mary in the story?' That was so wrong, Mary. That must have been so hard for you."

I would like my old friend to know that our encounter on the pool deck was a welcome and much-needed gift. Someone knew. She recognized and validated my pain. I was partially known.

Years later in my master's coursework on grief and trauma, I learned the name for the one of the feelings I was having: hopelessness. I had never had a feeling of hopelessness before my marriage. I certainly did not know the name for it.

Counselors, physicians, and researchers in many disciplines have described the many emotional and physical benefits that come from purposefully connecting with others when we walk through hurting places. Ira Byock, MD, an international leader and expert on palliative care, advises in his book *The Four Things That Matter Most:*

> *Isolation and abandonment cause suffering in people of all ages and cultures, even in the absence of illness. For all people under stress, dealing with illness, or facing change, emotional isolation can be torture. Far more than pain or any other physical symptom, isolation evokes a feeling of helplessness and hopelessness. This isn't only true when people are dying—it's true for everyone.* (p. 16)

It is most certainly true for anyone and everyone who is emotionally alone, isolated or in the dark.

7
THE RED (SCARLET) LETTER

On March 5, 2011, after my new experience of rejection from Bob #2, I sent the late-night email to my children that bulldozed the cemetery of secrets and emotions I had buried for four decades. The stories of my past were buried, yet not dormant, for buried stories never are. They are never inactive or inoperative or nondestructive. They continue to affect how we feel about ourselves and others, how we respond to life experiences, and how we interact with the world around us. Only two days after I clicked *SEND*, I was initiating contact with a psychologist to help me begin unearthing and prying open the coffins of my marriage chronicles. My first appointment on my way to well-being was set for March 21st.

A few days before my first appointment, I went shopping and out for dinner with a dear new friend of mine. In the marvelous mix of things, God intends all of us to stand ready to listen to the soul cry of others. As we sat at the restaurant sharing food and conversation, God provided an opportunity for us to share some of our life stories. As my friend shared some of her stories, I felt safe in sharing mine. This was another step in being vulnerable in order to be truly known.

As I left the Lakefront Wellness Center following my first meeting with Beth, I was gratefully aware of how safe I felt in sharing my stories. It was safe to be vulnerable there. My person was acknowledged and accepted. I felt a freedom I had not known before. The freedom, the "lift" I felt as I left her office, was a new and welcome experience for me. I had shared with Beth one of the deepest-buried secrets of my past, and by the second session, I was invading the carefully concealed sepulcher of my affair.

As I worked through this healing process, I learned that a husband engaging in polygamy will often encourage his wife to join him in the charade. As we dug up urn after urn of my cremated secrets, it became more and more apparent that this had been the case for me. Near the end times of our marriage, my husband was planning to take one of his employees, also a family friend, to Lake Venience for a professional conference. (She was actually the wife of Gary, who had encouraged me to do a triathlon.) I would have loved to have gone to Lake Venience, but I was not invited; and of course, I didn't insist upon it or voice any protest. Once again, I was passively submerging anger and shame, along with any other undefined feelings, while sabotaging any sense of self-worth or personal rights. Prior to the conference, my husband encouraged me to get together with Gary.

He had tried to get me to "swing" with him in couple relationships before. It wasn't until now, decades later, that I saw the complete picture and knew there even was a label for such a twisted, polygamist practice. I could now recall two other similar situations. There was the incident with our hearing impaired friends, Leslie and Rich. Why didn't he protect me? Why did he allow this treatment of me?

I see it now. He loved himself more.

He did not protect me then. He abused my love, my unconditional love for him. All these years I never told anyone in order to protect my husband. I continued in my silence to protect him and to protect my children. To me, my husband was intimidating. I did not feel emotionally safe to confront him. If I told him the blue sky was wonderful, he would convince me it was black. Some people who knew him from professional school said to me after our divorce, "Mary, you had to live in his shadow. That was how you had to survive."

As I wrote all of this, I would often stop and sort of moan silently. I would stop typing, rest my forehead on my right hand, and cover my eyes. This is not easy stuff to remember. It is not easy to put the pieces together and see the fuller picture of what was going on over the span of so many years. I had no idea that I was living in such denial.

My husband told me at some point during the divorce process that he would feel guilty for a while after having an affair, but soon desire the rush of a new relationship. So the other logical conclusion I had denied was that he did not love me enough to be faithful. He did not love me enough to be a loyal friend. He did not love me enough to protect me and stand by my side. And I was not enough for him. It was himself he loved more. He was a polygamist with a huge sense of entitlement. I believe he loved me, but it was a compartmentalized love. His love for me had limits. It was a love tagged, catalogued, and put in a box. In each conversation about other women, during every time they were in my home, during and after each affair, the sides of the box moved in closer and closer and his love grew more and more diluted. My death by emotional suffocation was imminent.

There was another occasion when Rita was still in the picture. (Well, I don't think she ever left. She probably is there still in some way or another.) But when my husband and Rita were with each other, Rita's husband came over to our apartment on Beloit Road. I was home alone with my daughter, a toddler at the time. Kids can sense when some people are not safe, or when they are not wild about kids. It is also likely that she was picking up on my messages of discomfort. But anyway, my little one kept her distance, as I did. I didn't know why he was there. I wanted him to leave. Maybe he also knew and was hurting about this damaging affair. Maybe he wanted to talk about it. He may have been pursuing me. Maybe Bob set it up hoping to create a swinging couple situation. I do not know why he came over to the apartment.

By the time of the Lake Venience conference, we were living in our last home together, the last year before we were separated. My husband was having or desiring yet another affair, and he had already encouraged me a number of times to share myself with his target's husband, Gary.

Yes, I did have an affair with the husband of my husband's desired lover at that time. I was attracted to him, an attraction never before allowed into the boundaries and framework of my married life. And do you now read the red letter I wore?

Here now was my destructive denial of self and mistaken idolatry of my husband. Now, I went so far as to cast aside my own values about relationships and the sanctity of marriage. When we lived in our second home, I had thrown out my Bible. I had denied all my feelings to a point of forgetting how to feel.

So I spent time with the husband of my husband's employee while she and my husband were together in a shared room in Lake Venience. This man was very handsome. He helped me feel pretty and desirable again. Someone was attracted to me. He noticed my athleticism, my intelligence, and my strength. I had already abandoned my love for God and my love for myself. Here I was, carrying out the hoped-for outcome of my husband, my idol, the person I lived and breathed for. I didn't know then that many others knew my husband was not faithful and had serial affairs. Some told me, "Well, it's about time! It's about time you had an affair!" But I felt awful. I felt ashamed and guilty. I hated what I had become.

I often reverted back to self-condemnation and to defending and protecting my husband. Even after the divorce and before I ever shared my story, my mother said to me, "I can't believe you are still defending Bob." I am realizing, in this phase of revisiting my marriage, that I am strong enough to go deeper than I ever have into the raw realities of the experience.

After my affair, I moved out of my home, for I couldn't stand what I had done. I was sick at heart. I told my husband that I would leave him for this other man. I thought someone wanted me. In truth, I wanted my husband, but I had to face the fact that the relationship was over. In truth, it was over before it began. My husband did not want me.

My psychologist is very attentive to my gestures and mannerisms, for they often can be a more accurate revelation of my feelings and emotions than the words I choose in the moment. As I shared with her what my husband had said during our divorce, that he knew I needed some man in my life to express myself and my sexuality; Beth noticed that I was rubbing, massaging my ring finger with my thumb. I was unconsciously, nonverbally expressing the truth that it was my husband I desired. "You were saying to me, 'I wanted Bob. I needed him in the fidelity of marriage.' You needed and desired the marriage, the fidelity of his love. You needed him." Bob was the man I wanted to share myself with and intended to have for my life on earth. I did not want another. "You wanted Bob and his fidelity."

And I would no longer share him with another. I had learned I was worth more than such treatment. For me, there was no turning back. One foot was on the pier, the other in the boat. I didn't know what was on the other shore. I knew what was on this side of the raging water. Even though it was painful and hurtful and would remain so here, I knew what to expect. Taking the boat across this stormy lake was dangerous, and I did not know what waited for me on the other side. The boat was beginning to drift away and I was now straddling the cold water. If I hesitated any longer, I would end up in the water without hope for rescue. I stepped fully into the boat.

During my session with my psychologist on October 31, we revisited the burial chamber of my affair. Beth commented that this session would be the darkest and the most difficult. The week before, she had asked that I look at the relationship I had with Gary from another perspective and recognize how even though wrong, it was used for positive outcomes.

The day and evening before, as well as the morning of my appointment, I had a sense of anxiety. My breathing felt labored, and I felt like I had nervous leg syndrome all over. I felt the need to take deep breaths. Drinking cold water felt good. The annoying feelings in my arms increased as I drove to Pewaukee for my appointment. I was early for my appointment, so I went to the coffee shop and drank two mugs of yummy coffee and had the last piece of pumpkin pie with a dollop of whipped cream.

For me, the affair wasn't about sex. It was a missing relationship. I fell in love with him. Entering into the affair did help me to let go of a relationship that was destroying me. I had suppressed so much of myself, including my anger, shame, and embarrassment as well as my dreams and preferences; I had forgotten how to feel. I could not let go of my husband. I had to learn that nothing was going to change. I wanted someone to love me like Bob loved his mistresses. I needed someone to validate me as a woman. I needed to see that I was lovable to someone.

My husband had encouraged me to have an affair with this man in so many conversations. He even said I must know I am a man's dream in bed. And I was going to believe that? In any case, I wasn't enough for my husband. Serial affairs are serial killers of a different kind.

When we were separated and I had moved out to an apartment with my children, my husband came over while the children were sleeping. He was still in a relationship with his mistress, and no doubt they were spending time together in the bed—*our* bed at *our* house. But my husband initiated sex with me. I cried in the middle of kissing the stars with great pleasure knowing that this would be the last time he would be inside of me. I had not expected him to come over and initiate this. He would not stop seeing his mistress, but still came over to my apartment to make love. He wanted to make love to me *physically*, anyway. I can't tell you why. But I still loved him. I wanted him to hold me, and now I see it brought in more confusion again. I remember now, how soon after his romantic visit I became determined to return to my house and reclaim what was mine, including my husband and my home.

As I shared this history with Beth, she said, "How confusing. *He loves me, he loves me not.*" Confusing, that's the word! That's the word that captures the effects of the emotional yo-yo I was riding. There were some positive experiences in my marriage. My husband treated me like his yo-yo on a string. He would pull me close and then let me down again and again and again. Often, he would leave me spinning at the end of the string. Well, now the string was tangled and knotted, and everyone knows that once that happens to a yo-yo, you have to cut the string. The wife, the yo-yo, rolls away, and the husband is left standing with a loop of string around his middle finger. He marries his mistress, who was just entering puberty when the wife was putting him through college and grad school.

After my then still husband's romantic visit to my apartment, I remember moving back to the house, and Mum saying, "You have to give it time." I slept on my usual side of the bed. When my husband didn't touch me that first night or the second, I moved onto the couch. I couldn't bear that.

The first night I slept on the bed, in the morning before he headed to the office, he got my toddler son from his bedroom and brought him to doze next to me for a bit. My husband said, "Well, *that's* the way it is supposed to be." Yes. I remembered it and wanted it, too. But I don't think we desired the same thing. He wanted to continue as it had been these many years. For him, this is the way it should be: You (meaning me), the loving wife at home, mother of my children—and you, the loving wife at home, forever my yo-yo. He wanted me back in the house, but he still would not be faithful. I had not returned to the home I desired, but back into his compartmentalized box of restricted love with no fresh air to breathe, while he was free to roam and still come home to my unconditional love.

My affair helped me to end my relationship with my husband. It was over, and I knew I wasn't going to stay in the marriage. For me to have an affair, I had already left Bob. I knew I couldn't go back. There was no going back. I could not, would not, be his not-so-precious yo-yo anymore.

Sex with my lover was incredible, spontaneous, and dynamic. Someone was attracted to me; some of the feelings long buried were back. I was set free to a degree, and I would get a rush just when he would kiss me. I saw that he was caring and that he admired me. He said I was so very dynamic. I had repressed so much of myself in my marriage. At that time, I was hoping the relationship would be more than it was. Beth said, "You fell in love." I said yeah. To me, he was very handsome. He was beautiful. He was in shape. I liked his face.

Beth posed the question, "Did it come to a place where you desired a man sexually more than your husband?"

"Yes, I guess I did."

She responded, "So did that happen for him? For Bob?

It was a question that required asking. I knew the answer to this question, a question I had never let myself think about all these years, let alone ponder the true, uncensored response.

"Yes. Bob came to a place where he desired someone more than me." I continued the natural curve of the question and answers. He had come to the place where he desired a number of women more than me. I was not enough.

Beth continued, "You were not having a sexual affair; you were having a relationship. You were completely starving. We all grasp and grab at things; desperate situations cause desperate measures. It doesn't justify your actions, but we are all capable of it. Try to recall what it was like to remember all these things from so long ago. Falling in love. You often revert to judgment and condemnation. You revert back to your religion sensors that close off or slam the door on the way to discovering what was it like to be Mary. The more honest you are and the more real you are, you will be of greater value in helping others. The more honest you are, the more aid, the more help you can impart to your readers."

As I was working hard to excavate these feelings, I would begin to judge and condemn myself before I had finished the excavation of, identification of, and explanation of my emotions. I would abandon the downward climb and not get to the bottom of it all. I wanted to escape back to the ledge.

The moment I typed this, I started to cry. I had buried my shame, my loneliness, my grief, my need to be loved, the need to be held, for a long, long time. And once again, I was at the ready to push it down, to hammer down my feelings now with the mallet of condemnation. Jesus would stay the blow. A broken reed he will not crush. Consider the adulteress who was facing a stoning by the self-righteous crowd. When Jesus challenged the men to pick up a stone to throw if indeed they had no sin, the malicious ones dropped their rocks. Drop the rock and pick up grace!

I had fallen in love with my lover, but at one point he dismissed the relationship and called it "just a game." I was devastated, like shattered glass. I wonder if that is what my husband thought of me, his wife. I wasn't just *playing* his wife. I *was* his wife. I have just realized that perhaps for him, our marriage *was* just a game. (This book is painful to write, yet I know God is going to do something magnificent with it beyond imagination. He will use the good, the bad, and the ugly.)

Not long after he had called it a game, the one I had an affair with wanted to get together again. He said he couldn't think of anything else.

The man I had fallen in love with went to counseling with his wife. He abruptly cut off the relationship with me. This was so unlike the way my husband treated me. My husband did not love me enough to do that for me. Why couldn't my husband stand by me and quit talking to his mistress? I wasn't good-looking enough or interesting enough as a wife *or* a mistress, I guess. I wasn't enough.

I ran into this one who now rejected me at the drug store. I told him I really hurt. He said a lot of people hurt. I said, "I am getting a divorce." He didn't say anything. A short time later, I saw his wife in the grocery store parking lot. I told her, while crying, that I was so sorry. It was a hard cry of true sorrow and regret.

I told my husband I would have left him for this man. I wanted my husband to want me like that. I told my husband I should never have married him. I said that because he had told me before we were even married that he would not be faithful. I had already lost him. I couldn't have either man, so I went on by myself. I was rejected by both. They are both married and had more children.

As I proofed my life experiences, now in black and white on the printed page, I asked myself, "Can rejection be any more apparent?" It was awful, and the depth of my silence for so long, very sad.

8

NOTHING BUT THE TRUTH?
SO HELP ME GOD!

A TEMPTATION TO CENSOR THE TRUTH

To censor is to edit, cut, or limit; to purge, stifle, or gag; to repress, suppress, or inhibit; to keep inside, bottle up, or hold back; to dominate, subdue, or overpower; to dismiss, drive out or throw out.

For all the actions listed above, a referee in the game of healthy living would call, *"Foul!"* Being authentic, being known, being *"insertive,"* and being truthful are the game winning plays.

Self-disclosure helps others to see you as human. People feel safe with others and appreciate others who let themselves be known.

The night before I met with Beth on April 4, 2011, when we entered into my issues with shame, denial, and reluctance to disclose, I had watched *Cat on a Hot Tin Roof* with my mother and father. It is a fantastic, four-star movie with Elizabeth Taylor and Paul Newman. The viewing of this movie, along with so many things going on around me, had such pertinence to what I was working through. To get into that drama, in and of itself, but also to view it and share the experience with my parents, as well as talking together after the movie about the emotional, social, and mental turmoil of what was going on, was relevant to the drama I was working through. The story was insightful.

Beth encouraged me to go back and recall what it was like to remember all these things again from so long ago, including falling in love. I needed to be ruthlessly honest. It was crucial. It had been a lot of hard work daring to leave the safety of the edge, climb downward into the crevasse, and chip out what had been preserved in ice and stone. Reverting to entombing the story again or tar-and-feathering myself would interfere with sharing the difficult truths of my experience. Who will roll away the stone?

We have worked hard to uncover my stories. If I begin to censor and select, stifle and reject, edit and suppress parts of the raw and real story and judge myself, reprimand myself, condemn myself, and send myself to jail; the real and fuller teaching of my story is lost again. Painting over the pain, whitewashing the stain, splashing KILZ on shame will send a message to others to keep silent at all costs. Healing will be unattainable.

When I was preparing to share my story that day, I was talking to myself in the shower. Tension and heaviness set in. So much for a relaxing shower. I am quick to condemn myself. Others may do the same. As I continued to prep myself for the day, I remembered this:

My intention was to write my story and share the downward climb so that others feel safe to share their stories and find personal validation, understanding, and healing. I want us to see the way out.

At long last, I have found it safe to let myself be vulnerable and share the truths about myself. It is too easy to put recall and writing in handcuffs in the name of law and order and back off. If I continue to condemn myself, I put a noose around my neck and choke the revelation of truth. Sealing a verdict of guilty at this point throws my self-protecting, vulnerable person back into solitary confinement once again. It is too easy to throw away the key, never to be heard from again.

DEALING WITH DIFFICULT TRUTH

It was November 14, 2011. My faithful friend Beth said she felt the need to bring up a difficult subject—maybe not now; maybe later. She advised that it would be okay to consider my work on the book when we met, but not to allow it to interfere with the therapy journey and its natural progression. She prayed. It was a powerful, Holy Spirit-led prayer.

Over the weekend and also during my drive out to the Lakefront Wellness Center, I sensed that God was keeping me mindful of the same concern. I saw myself once again diving into work goals and writing, at the possible expense of this therapeutic journey and of going deeper. Writing the book was a good thing, but could become a distraction. I now recognized that getting totally absorbed in other occupations was my chosen remedy for casting out difficult emotions.

Beth said, "I want to spend at least some time today, maybe more, dealing with Gary." She went on, "You experienced dual rejection. You were rejected by Bob and rejected by Gary." I had also betrayed myself, and I had betrayed God. She said, "You threw yourself into accomplishment. Where did you put all that rejection?" She followed with an answer. "You dealt with your feelings by throwing yourself into things wholeheartedly, so there wasn't room for despair."

As I recalled the affair, I commented again how Gary tried to let go of *it* but couldn't stop thinking about *it*. Beth picked up on my use of *it*. I had said *it* a few times. "Why *it*? What was it?" I had to wrestle a bit with the question. Why did I say *it*? Did I mean the physical relationship? No; *it* referred to *me*—*and* to the relationship. I don't know if Gary had used the word *it* or not. I can't remember. I just realized that I think *I* used *it* when I was writing about these events before. I said he couldn't stop thinking about *it,* not, "He couldn't stop thinking about *me*." That is sad.

Beth brought to light how using this word was "an incredible devaluation of self." I realized, in comparison, that I would say things like, "Why can't my husband let go of *her*?" I always referred to his mistresses as *her*; I referred to myself as *it*.

Beth clarified that relationships have many layers and levels. Gary had *agreed* to swap. It is not unusual for there to be different agendas, different needs at the same time, but at different levels. When Gary confronted Bob for taking Jill to Lake Venience and reserving only one room, there were more issues there than the obvious one. The situation was a threat to Gary's masculinity. A true alpha male can't let a challenge go unmet, even if he had agreed to the whole swap setup. The alpha male establishes sex privileges. In essence, Gary was telling me that in his hierarchy of females, I was second. Jill was his first. Gary had to fight for his first which very likely rekindled their relationship. Bob did not ever fight for me. For Bob, I was second. He did not want to lose me, but he did want to keep me compartmentalized in his life. In Bob's hierarchy I was second; I was second in both hierarchies. I had an affair at the prompting of my husband and I chose to do so out of a desperate need to climb out and validate myself, validate my attractiveness, and in the end, another rejection validated my sense of defectiveness.

Beth said, "One of the biggest reasons people have affairs is to be validated as a sexual being, validated as worthwhile. The mate has perhaps lost interest, and an affair initially holds promise for someone, holds value for the ego. In the end, it is a poisonous drink." I had followed the wrong path by not facing the despair and disillusionment Bob planted and cultivated. All human beings carry a sense of worthlessness; an ability to doubt is inherent in all of us. Bob kept deepening it.

Beth added, "Bob and Gary consented, at some time in some way, with each other. And you had huge denial with how Gary affected you. For Bob and Gary, it was practical polygamy with practical mistresses. It was essentially the playing out of a grand, intentional design Bob had long deliberated on. For Bob and Gary, it was a well thought out wife swap. But in the end, Gary was too threatened by Bob, and in addition, you were not a polygamist. Bob and Gary were polygamists. Gary could entertain the role of a polygamist without Jill knowing. Bob was okay with you knowing. He was a polygamist and was narcissistic enough. He had intentionally shaped the scenario. It is all profoundly complicated and an evolving of your acceptance of things. It was a plot of Bob's all along. The transformation of Gary and Jill and Bob and you involved a lot of effort and thought on Bob's part."

Beth had asked me how long I had known Gary and Jill before the affair. I shared how we knew them when we had our second apartment. I recalled that Gary and Bob actually worked together for a time. We must have known them for six years or so.

As I wrote this, I remembered another demeaning dynamic of it all. A dispatching scenario. Oh, puke. I had agreed to volunteer as a dispatcher for the company Bob and Gary worked for together. I volunteered for some night hours of dispatching from my home. I learned later that Jill did the same, but she got paid. I remember feeling used. I looked back now and recognized just one more example of how I let myself be exploited.

As I sat at my computer, I remembered my comments in another journal about how Bob showed an attraction to Jill way before Lake Venience. She was a friend, so I pushed the reality I witnessed away. And I thought he hadn't been cheating on me for the past few years. Now, decades later when I shared my story with a friend, I had forgotten that she had worked at the office, too. My friend explained how she had been aware of the relationship of my husband with Jill and later with Joan. I had not known that others knew about all or some of this. My friend added that way back then, Bob's relatives could not understand why I didn't leave him. They couldn't understand; I did not know they knew the story.

I recalled when I noticed how Bob and his next mistress reacted to each another while I was at the office one day (so many years ago). Joan perhaps thought I did not see the nonverbal cue. It was not very subtle. I thought the affairs were over.

(I hate this. I really am tired. It is late, and as I type this, I remember more. I can even see the gesture now and the office area. I feel like I need to cry. *Dear God, I would never, never go through those times again. Dear God—I wasn't blind. I wasn't stupid.* There's more; but enough. I can't write about more sad stuff. Oh, and this. I actually made love with my husband in his office. Shit. That is all I want to say about his office, one I worked for and supported to make it a reality. A different day, before Joan or Jill worked there, I went into the office when everyone was gone. I scrubbed the floors and cleaned out the lab area and the mess where everyone must have had lunch. I remembered this now. Another professional stopped by and I said Bob wasn't there. He seemed to smile and laugh a bit as he looked at me scrubbing the tiled floor at the entrance to the office. And now as I read this passage once again for editing, I can identify the name for what I was feeling that day when I was on my knees with a scrubbing rag and bucket. It was shame. Yes, I felt shame, but I pushed it down. Buried shame does not decompose underground. It thrives and poisons the soul. Now, I am not swearing; I am not crying out loud. But I am very sad.)

THE THREE R'S: REJECTION, REJECTION, AND REJECTION

I went to Lincoln Grade School. We played tetherball, dodgeball, kickball, hopscotch, and bombardment. We studied the three R's: reading, 'riting, and 'rithmetic. I think I was in sixth grade when "arithmetic" became "mathematics." We called it "the New Math." Now completing the sixth decade of my life, I am wrestling with a different set of "three R's": rejection, rejection, and rejection.

I experienced rejection in two relationships, as well as my betrayal of self and my betrayal of God. I was second in the hierarchies of both men. As we all do, I carried a sense of worthlessness. Bob intensified it. I remember Beth saying that Bob was broken. He was. Perhaps he still is. What <u>did</u> I do with that rejection?

As I wrote and rewrote about rejection, thoughts and memories of how I devalued myself spun around and around in my head. It was as if the devaluation of me and rejection were braided together. Yes, braided together in a downward spiral.

When I was mistreated, I buried the emotions and accepted a more negative self-image. When I was rejected, I buried the emotions and concluded that I was not enough. When I let go of my dreams, I discarded part of myself. When I let go of my friends, I was snubbing myself and my friends. When I never introduced friends into the relationship, I climbed into a trench to hide myself. There seemed to be walls, and I was on the outside of them. I retreated from social engagement. What happened to me? When I denied my values, I was rebuffing my very self. Where did the rejection start? When did devaluing begin?

I was just becoming popular in high school. And guys were taking a second look. Bob came onto the scene and pursued me. He was very jealous. Things turned around, and not in a healthy way. Why? How and why did I relinquish control? What the hell happened? Why did I forfeit myself? Shame, silence, denial, and diminishing identity were knotted in the braid spiraling out of sight. There was now a pervasive inferiority, a consuming worthlessness, a slow erosion of self. To disguise the bridal rejection, so I could not see it or dwell on it, I concealed the painful marital masquerade in laudable accomplishment in athletics and academia.

While I was still married and before the birth of two of my children, I cut my wedding dress; I shortened it to wear for Easter one year. I cried the whole time I was doing it. I was once a bride, and now I was rejected. The rejection was awful, and I kept it all to myself for forty years. I wore my shame. I wore my shame on Easter Sunday. The drastic alteration of my wedding dress dramatically symbolized the ugly transformation from the procession of a beautiful bride down the center aisle of a church building to the humiliation of a young wife.

One day in our flat, I was looking in the mirror in our bedroom. I said, "Look how long my hair is! I look pretty, kind of pretty now, don't I?" Bob was lying in bed. He responded, "You should get it cut short." I remember feeling sad that he had said that. Surprised he had said that. He always had liked it long. Later, I felt troubled that he didn't want me to possibly be pretty to someone else, attractive to anyone, or he just didn't want me to feel pretty. His response made no sense to me. Maybe he did not like my longer hair now. Even with long hair, I still wasn't pretty to him anymore.

Why did I maintain the silence? Why didn't I ask why? I was despairing, but didn't pause to recognize it. *God, show me, reveal to me, so I can heal, grow strong in you and use me to write and teach and help others. Change what needs changing.* **Write!**

A week or so later, I was reading some verses from the book of Isaiah in the Old Testament. The verses that grabbed my heartstrings and played a tune of validation were these:

Fear not, for you will not be ashamed; be not confounded, for you will not be disgraced, for you will forget the shame of your youth. (Isaiah 54:4 ESV)

The Lord will call you back as if you were a wife deserted and distressed in spirit—a wife who married young, only to be rejected," says your God. (Isaiah 54:6)

As I read and then reread these verses, it became so apparent that God understood the distress and the despair of a young wife rejected. God knows. He understands. He was comparing the distress and abandonment of the nation of Israel in dire circumstances to a young wife in despair. Our Redeemer understands. The passage goes on to talk about God's everlasting kindness, unfailing love, covenant of peace, and his compassion. God knew and knows my heart's cry.

As I have noted, I saw that when I was supported in becoming vulnerable and authentic by sharing my story, others felt encouraged to do likewise. I shared my story of rejection with a dear friend. My friend had suspected that her relative was a victim of verbal abuse. She shared with her relative that I had gone through so much and was just finally talking about it now. The relative disclosed that she had experienced unrelenting verbal abuse for decades as well as physical abuse. A door opened, and another once-quiet voice risked being known and welcomed compassion in.

The next November day, I joined Beth for one of our sessions and she quickly sensed I was a little sad, agitated even. She opened our time together with prayer. It was beautiful, truly Holy Spirit-led. She prayed for clear perceptions, guidance, comfort, and peace. She prayed for me to let go of shame. Beth spoke of my denial of rejection in my marriage. I had also noted that the end of my recent, brief relationship with "Bob #2" from the dating service was like a post-traumatic stress event where the rejection of the past raised its ugly head and demanded my attention.

I had denied all the rejection from Bob and Gary and of my own betrayal of self and of God. "It is difficult for you to consider that Bob planned out the situation with Jill and Gary," Beth noted. My own self-respect and sense of value were dragged under by the strong current of rejection and destructive schemes. [My evaluation of the swap was separated by thirty-eight to forty years. I did not consciously understand the dynamics before my downward climb.]

A TRAGIC FLAW: VULNERABILITY TO LOSE MY IDENTITY

"You had a vulnerability to losing your identity in someone else," Beth observed. "You were attracted to someone who would dominate you. You subsequently lost the identity you were just developing, a weakness. You have a vulnerability to the leading and influence of others. The draw for you was Bob's strength and ability. Dependency was appealing, and in that, you lost yourself. God allows failure to expose us to ourselves. Look how easily you are lost to yourself! With enough pressure and influence, you lose your identity. And apart from God, you are incomplete."

My friend continued, "It is an amazing dichotomy: You were dependent and voiceless, yet also demonstrating the epitome of strength, human strength, in academics and athletics. You were a triathlete and also one who climbs mountains. You summited Mt. Kilimanjaro. In neither extreme did you find a solution. *You could not achieve out of disillusionment.* You claimed, 'I will march and move on alone and triumph on my own.' This does not remedy the self-respect you lost. It isn't going to resurrect your sense of value and self-respect."

"Mary, you had many woundings. Spend time with these woundings!"

She reminded me, "In your story of George, you stated to yourself and out loud, 'I'll be alone again.'"

George was someone I had met about five years after my divorce. Yet at the time, I had not consciously recognized that my relationship with George would not be very different from my relationship with Bob. Even though I was not fully aware of the risk of repeating the past, I was scared. God was extending protection even though I was not conscious of how a marriage with George would mirror my previous marriage that demanded that I lose myself. So there was a very present fear that I would lose myself again. I remembered how awful, distressful, and lonely I felt as Bob's wife. I remembered how it felt to lose myself.

Sitting at a table at a coffee shop after this session, I stopped to pray: *Lord, how do you want me to handle this? How do I grieve this loss? Forfeiting myself, loss of self-respect, loss of identity, wounding, rejection, disillusionment? How do I? Can you? Can you mine this rejection heap and help me heal? Heal me, Lord!*

Beth commented that George's denial of the existence of any God forecasted that he would have been even more narcissistic, gravely narcissistic. We were both almost thinking the same thing at the same time, once again. When I had said earlier that George was divorced (and that his wife had wanted it), Beth had asked why. I had never asked George, but I had thought that his ex probably had ended the marriage because she had lost herself under George's control and regimen and needed to find herself again. At this point, I said that it was interesting and revealing that I had interpolated that as the reason. Yes, I had a concern about losing myself again.

I had a fear of losing my identity and losing my freedom to be and live out all I was meant to be. I had and have a dread of this dependency I was vulnerable to.

Beth pointed out how I let go of George as I remembered what it was like before in my marriage. I was afraid of losing myself again and becoming dependent on someone else who would dominate and control, afraid of a loss of freedom to be and live out myself.

That day after reading over my session notes, I asked myself, "What does self-respect look like?

WHY DO I WANT TO GET MARRIED AGAIN?

The first week in December 2011, I was looking through my files for one thing or another, tax information perhaps. I discovered some old pictures. They were pictures from high school, pictures of Bob and me when we were on the debate team. I thought I looked pretty. Bob and I looked so very young. We <u>were</u> very young. And to think we got married only a year or two later. I said to myself, "Yes, I do think I was pretty then."

Why did I want to get married again? Beth and I talked about it. I had been divorced for twenty-eight years and was independent and self-sufficient. Beth said, "You were deeply disillusioned to stay single for so long. You were profoundly disillusioned and you retreated. What could possibly change that for you to consider risking again?"

Check out the timing! I raised my children; they were raising their children now. My grandchildren were growing up; my parents were growing older. I was facing a time in life when I would lose my parents. They played a huge role in my life. I had watched them grow old together. And, I was living in the upper flat of my family home. It was a place of safety. I had retired from my career with the YMCA, a more than full-time role. The roles I played were changing, and I felt the desire to grow old with someone.

I also have a huge desire to be held. I want to enjoy and share my sexuality with someone, a husband who truly loves me, even cherishes me. I am growing older, too, but I'm not looking for someone to take care of me or provide for me. I want a life companion.

We closed our session in prayer. Beth prayed for my courage to write and for God to guide my writing. It was important for me to write about rejection, but I seemed to have been avoiding writing for the last few weeks.

During the session I talked about my fortieth high school reunion the preceding fall. My high school debate coach was there. He told me that when he had run into one of my college professors way back when, he remembered the professor saying, "And can she write!" (These thoughts took me back to my college years after my divorce and the relationship experiences I had then.) At the reunion, I ran into one of my high school boyfriends. I really liked him a lot. It was a very meaningful reconnection. Another classmate had said he had a crush on me for the last two years of high school. He thought I was so very pretty. "You're still pretty." That was a magical gift.

As I was exploring the question of why I wanted to remarry, I went back through some earlier journal entries: On May 5, 2011, I had joined two very dear friends for lunch, two women I loved and deeply respected. For a number of years, we had coached women, men, and families, especially in cross-cultural communication, to equip them for short-term missions. As we talked and ate at the Indian restaurant, a cuisine we all truly enjoyed, I shared my story. Leanne said to me as we walked back to the buffet table, "I knew there was a story. I always sensed, knew there was something, a story down deep in you." Ginny commented that the current events surrounding Maria Shriver and the long-hidden betrayal by her husband, Arnold Schwarzenegger, must have really hit me. She was right. I wanted to talk with Maria and encourage her in some way.

I also shared the story of how I had walked out on Raul at the wine bar, telling him "It's over!" I shared with them how my psychologist had explained that my action was transference of the Bob situation onto Raul. It was me telling Bob it was over. I told them how I had apologized to Raul. They understood, and that felt good.

As I shared my stories, they listened with compassion. They didn't see my reactions as negative, but as hugely understandable. Ginny shared some stories about her childhood, and Leanne shared a story about a woman she knew whose husband had died and left her with an oppressive debt he had not been honest about. He had led her to believe it had all been taken care of long ago. Abuse and betrayal were not unknown to them.

Later in the day, I watched one of my grandchildren in a track race and watched another play her violin at a school event. It was great fun and a welcome break. That night, I was very tired. The day had been rough in many ways. Traveling back into the past to share my story had churned up sadness and depressing recollections. There were many similarities between my experiences and those of the celebrity wife. Her story made the newspaper, but her pain was made far more public than mine. I ached for her and could empathize with her pain. It was splashed on newspapers and across television screens. My own rejection, lack of being appreciated, embarrassment, marriage farce, shame, and betrayal had been printed in black and white in the daily journal so many years ago for the entire city and state to see.

How many mistresses had known my husband in my home, in my bed, even when I was in the hospital after the delivery of my children? Six affairs, probably more, over ten years. Deception, lies, and betrayal. He had told me he wanted to have a baby with another woman. I worked to put him through undergrad and grad school, and now someone who was just entering puberty when I was doing all that was reaping the benefits of all my hard work.

Even now, after being married to my ex-husband and having two children of her own, Bob's mistress has never acknowledged that what she did was wrong. I wonder if she has ever paused to think how desperately awful it was not to have my children with me six months out of the year. You would think there would be some sort of empathy. She did not care then and I have no reason to believe that she cares now. My husband never cared. None of this matters to him.

Lord, Lord! What am I to do with all of this? Revisiting and knowing all of these draining emotions and loss of self? It was a faceoff with betrayal, shame, embarrassment, sadness, grief, anger, rejection, repression, and oppression. It was climbing down into this brutally cold crevasse where I had to chip through the thick layers of denial and look at these truths with a high-powered headlamp: I was lied to and deceived. My person was ignored, not valued, not appreciated. I was disregarded as the mother of my children. I was not loved. I was cast aside, not celebrated, not supported, and not cared for. I felt heaviness as I climbed deeper still.

Through all of this hell, all of these years, I really thought I was held by someone who loved me. How could I think that? I know now that I was in denial since I was nineteen. My love for him was unconditional. Why? Why? Why? Why did I put up with it?

I will not be treated like that again. I will not be disregarded. I will not tolerate being ignored. I will not accept deception and lies. I will not endure betrayal, unfaithfulness, lies, ugly control, oppressive language and behavior, ridicule, shame, or lack of support.

I am wise in God. I will hold out and up what I discern. I will not question myself. I will not deny my feelings, perceptions, discernment or my self-worth. I will take to heart and soul that I was made in the image of God and he loves me as his daughter.

I will insert myself into the situation. I am and will be significant. Apart from God, I can do nothing. Apart from you, Bob, I will be just fine!

Along with these formerly unnamed emotions, I had buried broken-ness, weakness, and failure. I can no longer deny all of this reality buried long ago and I cannot deny how this past affects my present.

Lord, I want these deep and long-buried layers to be touched by you. I receive my circumstances as a gift from you. I want to meet you in this journey into the deep of my soul. You are creating a way for me to be more vulnerable. I am safe in your love and know now I am safe in the love of the many beautiful friends and family you have surrounded me with. This is a great gift. You do this all for my good; let me use it for your glory.

Beth helped me to see that lying about or suppressing my feelings is, in a way, bearing false witness of myself. I didn't know I was doing that. I did not know then how to do otherwise. Yes, I was lying as well. I liked "reading, 'riting and 'rithmetic" and excelled in them. Rejection, rejection, and rejection I tried to excel out of, but that didn't work. Striving for excellence and accomplishment did not resurrect my sense of self-worth. And for the record, I dislike rejection.

IT'S HOW YOU DO LOVE

I sat on the beach for a while before meeting at the Lakefront Wellness Center. The wind was refreshing. The waves rolling softly, then crashing into shore; the smell of lake water; the pleasant sound of children play-ing in the background; someone playing bongo drums on the sidewalk nearby; the slight cool of wind on my arms and the warm sun on my face; all were a lovely and pleasing blend of sights, sounds, and smells that together made me happy. I was content.

Beth had given me another homework assignment: How and what love did Bob show me? What was it?

I saw a remarkable investment of myself. Affair after affair, hurt after hurt, as I denied myself and my feelings I invested more and more of myself into the relationship. It was a high price that I paid. I gave more and more and became less and less.

"You take huge risks for love, Mary. You regard family and marriage as very important and valued. It was not denial or naiveté. *It is how you do love.*"

I realized that my love didn't matter to Bob. I wanted him to say, "Mary always stood beside me." But he didn't, and he won't.

Then I started to develop a renewed confidence. I was swimming, running, and biking. I felt like I was looking pretty. I had taken a writing course in children's literature. I was regaining some confidence in myself. Bob was pushing "swinging" again. I could describe the scenarios, but didn't have a name for it before. As I mentioned, Beth surmised that perhaps it was his way to keep me. I recalled his severe jealousy in high school. How ironic. You don't keep a woman by treating her like garbage and discarding her. Beth had said he very well may have thought that if I joined him in his swinging, I would stay. It was another way to control and hold me, especially as I was growing more and more confident. I again remembered the time I thought my hair looked pretty and Bob said I should get it cut. That was just another reflection of his possessiveness, jealousy, and controlling behavior. I remember how he almost gave me pointers on getting together with Gary.

———————————

What held me? What feeling of love or sense of love kept me there?

———————————

I sometimes felt pretty when I was riding my bike. Pulling my daughters in a bugger trailer all summer, I really had slimmed down. We rode to Door County, biking seventy to ninety miles a day. I ran across a picture of me getting ready to head out for a ride. I was wearing short shorts. I *did* look good in my short shorts. I was pretty. But I was not enough.

I think it was more my strength and unconditional love for Bob that held me, no matter what. He was the man I loved, the one I married, the one I gave myself to. The one for whom I gave up my scholarship, my high school band trip, my friends, high school involvement, a summer in Germany, my dream of a PhD, my legs, my health. Every time I was betrayed, I held on, denied myself, and invested more of myself. It *is* how I do love. I was always loved, always safe, always cared for, always valued in my childhood home. Unconditional love is the environment of relationship I grew up in.

When we were just starting college, I remember Bob's mother saying to him, "You're not married yet." She said this as Bob was going out when I couldn't. I thought he was just going out with the gang from work. As I look back now, I wonder if he was already unfaithful to the relationship. Did Mum see something I didn't see? Did she know something I didn't know?

The women Bob had affairs with he brought to our apartment. Actually, I am realizing that he was probably having affairs continuously. Everything was running together. If he ever really did feel guilty, it wasn't for very long. I remembered just now: I was twenty and in labor with our first child. In the middle of some wild contraction, Bob started telling me how bad he felt. I recall thinking to myself, "I can't handle this now!"

When I was pregnant, he had an affair with a woman from work. I don't know if they were ever actually together in our first home; I never thought about that until now. In our second apartment, there was the girl from Australia, and Rita—that I know of. He brought them both into our home. He was involved with the girl from Australia before, during, and after my second pregnancy. He wanted to go to Canada with her. (I actually said no.) He was having an affair with Australia when he told me to stay in the hospital longer, even though the doctor was ready to send me home. He wanted more time with his mistress in *my* bed.

It seems he was with Rita and the girl from Australia at the same time. The girl from Australia was over at the apartment when I was home. My husband handed my baby daughter to her, to his mistress, to give my baby girl a bottle. I recently apologized to Katy for not intervening and telling Miss Australia to get the hell out of my home. I was upset that she was letting air get into the nipple of the bottle and I said nothing. It is very difficult to recall all of these events. It is sad and sickening.

When I edited this copy on the computer, I wished I could be an angel standing by to gently remove precious little Katy from the arms of my husband's mistress and place her in the arms of young Mary. I would kiss the sweet baby girl and sit next to Mary and tell her, "You and your children are worth more than this. I will send your husband and his mistress away. They will not come back."

When we went to Door County one summer, I was considering divorcing Bob. We only had our two daughters at that time. We had an argument at the beach at Weborg Point.

Sometime later I found the torn-up letter from Rita in our third home. I concluded he was still seeing her. This was also where he told me about and read the letter from Leslie that discussed their relationship/affair that he simultaneously denied. And this is where he was trying to get me to swing with Rich, Leslie's husband. Now I think he was having relationships with all three women while we were living there. Then there were Jill and Joan, who I think were working at the office at about the same time. So, it appears that for a good part of our marriage, he was cheating on me—and, I guess you could say, also cheating on the women he was having affairs with.

My mother said to me once after our divorce, "You loved Bob so much, Mary; you will always love him." He was going to be my husband forever.

Not until I worked through therapy and wrote this book, could I say I do not love him anymore. I do not love him in any way anymore. He was a jerk, an ass, a liar, a betrayer, a cheater, a user, a loser. He lost me! How big a loser can you be? This is but part of my journey.

What was it that held me? What was it that trapped me? *How could the love I had for him be a trap for me?* What did he give me? What did he sacrifice?

When we lived in our second home, before the birth of our second child, I asked him to wait before he jumped into graduate school. We needed to spend some time together and I was convinced in my own mind and heart that if he only waited, an opportunity would show up for him to continue to pursue his dream. I was sad that he released his grip on his longtime dream. It hurt even more to realize that he didn't regard our relationship as important enough to wait to make his next step. Now facing my denial, of course, I realize he had let go of the relationship long before this stage. (Another radical and sarcastic thought: maybe if he had not been cheating on me, he would have had more time for his studies.)

He means nothing to me now. Nothing.

I was thinking as I was sitting on the beach today that Joan, his last mistress when he was my husband, must not have understood what kind of man he was. After all, he said to my children: *"Your mother* wanted a divorce."* (And he tells them that to this day.) Yes, I was backed into a corner for so long, but he wouldn't divorce me. Yet he wouldn't be faithful. After Joan, it would be someone else. I wonder if Joan ever pondered this. All those women having affairs with Bob were lying to themselves as well. She had to lie to herself just as all the others did. I wasn't the only dumb one. Well, yes, this is very true: I didn't let myself think about the whole network of affairs until forty years after it all started.

I was his wife. I was Mary. And he was not going to leave me. What am I saying? He left me a long time ago. Or maybe this was his way of leaving. I remember reading once that this is often what happens. The man backs the woman into the corner. In any case, I said *Enough.* I quit.

And now I see and say: I won. I won my freedom to be the woman and the mother God made me to be.

I win. I graduated from college with honors and also earned my master's; in so doing, I developed my gifts and talents to pursue the dreams God intended for me. I win. I achieved career excellence. I win. I have the blessed gift of three beautiful children and five grandchildren.

I never really needed you. You brought upon me heartache, pain, and disaster. My children were conceived in unconditional love. In his great grace, God gave me children. They are amazing. They are my best friends. They alone are worth the pain and suffering I endured. For them only would I live this life. You are a liar, a deceiver, a betrayer of love, faith, trust, and sacrifice. I truly would like to never see you again. I intend to avoid seeing you.

I give my sacrifice up to the lives of my three children and their spouses and the five and any other grandchildren that come hereafter. I withdraw my sacrifice for you for your success, for your dreams. The six plus five (and then some) alone are worthy of my sacrifices. I loved you unconditionally and you betrayed me wholeheartedly.

I kept myself in bondage to my husband's life, serving that hope, serving this idea of him loving me. I made him my idol and let myself be assumed into his identity.

At the end of our May 23, 2011 session, Beth asked me if I thought Bob would be willing to get together and talk. Without any hesitation, I said no. Not too long ago, he refused to say he was sorry. Even now, he won't say he is sorry for these offenses. He doesn't usually acknowledge my presence if we are in the same room.

The morning before all of this, I thought back on my YMCA career and how I was loved. I considered all the wonderful things over the past twenty-plus years and how my oldest daughter said, "Mom, we all aspire to be like you," and then listed all the things God has let me be and do. Wow. And I remembered my retirement party and listened again to the message from Joy that I had saved on my old answering machine. I have been greatly blessed, beyond all expectations.

9
AN AMAZING CHOREOGRAPHY OF PAST, PRESENT, AND FUTURE

One morning I wrote in my journal, "I could visit the four homes we lived in as well as East High School. I could go back and visit young Mary who lived there, who grew up there. I talked with Dr. Beth about the idea; she said it was *brilliant*.

On a summer day in 2011, I rode my bike five miles from Hillside Drive where my country ride usually begins. I took College Avenue to Grange, then back on Grange to College and the neighborhood school. From there, I cranked out to my favorite farm just beyond Hill Top Road. I crossed Crowbar and rode on and on... The bike ride was grueling. It was great. There were lots of the old, tough hills. "The old grey mare, she's just what she used to be!" Ha! And stronger, I would say. I was actually able to tackle all the hills of my bike routes from years gone by. After my ride, I threw my bike in the back of the car and drove to Menard Drive and our fourth home. The mature trees were large and very pretty. I was happy to see that the old crab apple tree still stands, one of the most beautiful crab apple trees I have ever seen.

My son was born there. I became a runner and a triathlete. I still remember running mile after mile around the huge surrounding block and checking on the kids after each lap. I trained for and finished three triathlons. I raised my kids in that home; it was a joy and tons of fun. In that place, they became my three dearest friends.

When I lived on Menard Drive, I completed my bachelor's degree and began my career at the YMCA. This was my home when I threw out the baby Jesus and about six years later on May 4, 1989 asked God back into my life. I was a part of a new church plant when I lived here. I worked through divorce; I changed my last name. I fell in love with George and let go of the relationship with George.

For the first five years or so when I lived there, I thought my husband was faithful to me. I am sure now that I was mistaken. There were two or three I knew of later, anyway. What was it like to be alone yet determined, grieving and suicidal, hitting bottom and simply taking the next step? I lived a lot of life in this place.

One evening after the divorce, I shared dinner and conversation with my three children. I suggested, "Let's go around the dinner table and each of us tell what we admire most about all the other family members here."

Joy said, "Mom has made a new life for herself."

On a late afternoon, I was sitting on the picnic table on our backyard patio. I was drinking a cup of coffee out of one of those free mugs from a gas station long ago. It was a black-pleated bottomed mug of matte olive green glass. My daughters had just arrived home on the bus. Katy raced up the driveway and found me in the backyard. "Are you sad, Mom? You look sad. Are you thinking about the divorce?"

"Yes, Sweets, I am sad and I am thinking about the divorce."

I cut the grass, shoveled the snow, fixed the pool, changed the oil on the car, went to college, and worked at the Y. I took one daughter to swim practice, one to Scouts, and shot hoops with my son. The kids climbed trees, went sledding from the back hill to the front yard into the ditch by the road, and swung on the swing set. Later, I moved into an apartment. I couldn't afford the house anymore and couldn't afford the time to take care of it. Seems like I remember a different Mary back then. I kicked

Bob out of the house when he shoved me around the kitchen. I recall excruciatingly sad memories and fun and joyful memories. Bob's second car accident. I remember that during weather with a forty-below wind-chill, I took the car in for repairs and then ran the few miles home. Got a cat. There was happy and there was a lot of sad. There was a lot of hard work. When I was in college, I would let myself get five hours of sleep and start the new day. Eventually I took it to five and a half. It was a grueling pace. It was tough. So long ago. It seems so very long ago...

That article in the Journal.

I hit the bottom and God brought about new growth and gains in physical, mental, social and spiritual well-being and strength. I received a New International Version (NIV) Bible for Mother's Day from my kids in May 1989. (While I was visiting Menard Drive during my trek back in time, I prayed Psalm 139 and the scripture I call my life verse: Psalm 119:30–32.)

I sold my engagement and wedding ring when I lived there and put the eighty dollars toward a pair of cross-country racing skis. I was going to try something new. I was really sad when I went to a jeweler to sell my ring. I was going to say it was heartbreaking, but my heart was already broken.

A few days after the bike ride to my old home on Menard Drive, I met with Beth. I told her a lot had happened the past week and that I had a lot to share. Beth asked me to share the prayers God had given me. I read and prayed the prayers I had included in some previous journal entries. Beth asked me to return to one about being honest. "Keep me completely gentle and humble, kind and at the same time just, truthful, authentic, and patient." Beth saw a heart of surrender in my prayers, she said.

I told Beth I was in a deep place of my past. I visited my high school, our first apartment on Miller Place, the second home on Beloit Road, the Flat, and Menard Drive. Beth perceived how I had become inauthentic in high school as I told her about all the things I had been striving for since I was a little one, a page-long list of things, and how I had let go of all of them.

I shared some of the stories from my past, including the time when I was pregnant and went dancing with my husband, who also invited his girlfriend. And the story of Bob and his last mistress teasing and laughing with each other outside the huge window of the school pool deck for all the parents sitting on the bleachers to see. And the story of the party when he seemed anxious to make sure all his friends at the gathering knew I was his wife. The method and timing of his interruptions and the way he introduced me multiple times in such a hurried manner gave me an impression that there was some imperative behind his action. He was introducing me hurriedly so everyone was clear that this time he had brought his wife along. *Those times were some of the most inauthentic stages of my life; times of great shame and embarrassment.* I see now how I did not stand up for my rights. I let myself be shamed. These stories all took place on a public stage. My humiliation affected me, but I denied it and tried to push it away. I did not confront the hurt and did not confront the one causing the hurt.

I saw Bob for who he really was as I walked the places of the past. I saw how alone I was; the scenes of the past made me sick at heart.

Beth said, "You were silent because of Bob's need for protection and your need to present a certain look to the world. The truth was too difficult, too unspeakable, too shameful. Silence kept it contained."

I then shared with Beth how I had at last shared my story with my mother and father. I cried out loud and hard as I explained how Mom and Dad had leaned in, in loving attentiveness to my story. They hadn't known. Why hadn't I shared it with them? *Thank you for having confidence in us,* they had told me. "What a perfect response," Beth remarked. Beth asked that I give Mom and Dad a hug and kiss for her.

I had falsely assumed that Mom and Dad had too much to handle in their lives at this point in time. I had incorrectly imagined what they might say: "That is the past and it is over. You don't need help." Not so. They didn't say that at all!

This was when Beth said she was convinced that Bob was a polygamist and that he wanted me to join in and be accepting of it.

Beth said, "You need to know you look good. You are in shape." We talked about how we all have "rolls" at older ages.

I looked out at Pewaukee Lake after my appointment. It was beautiful and sunny now. It had been cloudy when I drove out, and then it had rained. As I sat outside in front of the cantina, under an umbrella, I looked out on the lake. Jesus was walking on the water, smiling, even laughing. He was so happy, yes, gleeful. He was not calming waves or storm; he was happy and laughing and smiling with me. Everything is okay now. Everything is all right.

Here is another thing. I decided to share my story with a friend who had known me years ago. We were connecting more again because of similar involvements. I learned in the process of sharing my story that just recently, another friend from the past had spoken negatively of me. She had drawn conclusions based on only partial knowledge. The old friend I was reconnecting with had been influenced by this opinion, but was now reconsidering her evaluation of me. She thought maybe she had never known me. She later realized that I was the Mary she had always known. I shared the good, the bad, and the ugly, and she knew I was still Mary.

On June 28, 2011 I had written: *I was in an abusive relationship. Bob abused me.* This is the first time I had said this, realized this. It is the first time I realized it was so. His controlling behavior, including his affairs, his jealousy, and his negating and disaffirming speech was emotionally life-threatening. Over the previous three months, walking and talking through the experiences of my buried past, I was moved to come to terms with the painful reality that my husband had not loved, valued, or respected me. He didn't love me, and I wasn't enough.

I remembered. I remembered some decades earlier when I was dating someone after the divorce. I liked him a lot and he was quite handsome. I fell in love with him. One day he asked me, "Why did you and your ex get a divorce?" I can't remember what I said, if anything, but essentially I told him nothing. Maybe I said it was a long story—some sort of short answer that doesn't fill in any information. After a reflective moment, he responded to my nonanswer (a kind of silence) with, "He abused your goodness."

I will grab hold of God's promise of personal deliverance. He is faithful. I can just look and see how even as of late; he has been bringing things together, an amazing choreography of my past, present, and future.

As I was reading a draft of my story in my living room in the flat, I looked around the room and realized that the room is, in fact, an expression of me, including delightful contributions from my kids and many things from my travels. Every room actually has a Mary's touch and flair. That was not the case in any of the homes when I was married. I was not recognizable there.

When did I cry? I didn't remember crying all those years… Yes. I did cry during the pre-natal classes and when I was cutting my wedding dress.

During my journey into my past, I have heard stories from others who have traveled through similar places and are moving toward recovery. I have heard other stories, different in some ways, yet similar accounts of brokenness, sadness, and hopelessness.

———————————————

God—what book do you want me to write? When someone is despairing, it is life-sparing to discover that someone understands.

———————————————

When someone is hurting in their brokenness and wounding, it is life-giving to read an article or book that somehow, in some way, expresses their own experience. When someone is lost and shamed and alone, it is an emancipation of the heart to be heard with compassion, mercy, and grace. It is good to know that we do matter to others and that we matter to God.

Who do I need to reach out to? Who do I need to be available to? Where do I need to insert myself? Why do we not insert ourselves? Especially me, now, for the children who have no voice.

Babies dying, children crying, people starving, people living without knowing they are loved by God.

Here's an important thing: We must keep it safe for our children to return to our hearts when things go wrong. When things go wrong, when things get tough, we must keep it safe for our children to come home where love, safety, and security are certain. Don't leave her or him without a safe heart to return to.

I know I needed this journey to become authentic. And if I can get honest with myself and God and others and release the past for his sake, God will unleash authentic power in my preaching, writing, and activism. I am more fully available to and for God's purposes.

Lord, use me as you would. Unleash in me all that you are, so I may freely be an instrument of your truth, your story, your love, your grace, your peace. In your name and for Your Name's Sake I will not back down. Use me, Lord.

Lord, may I stand in your counsel. May I sit by your feet and proclaim your words to your people. May I insert myself into the circumstances, situations, and life environments you put me in with your love and grace, mercy, and goodness, remaining humble in your tender care. Lord, may I speak your word faithfully. God, protect me so that I may remain what you created me to be. In you I find my true identity and in you I have the true freedom to be all that I can be.

Make me "nourishment" for others. Mold me and shape me for your kingdom purposes. This is the day you have made. Let me, let us, rejoice and be glad in it. May I, in your wisdom and strength, defend the cause of the poor and of those in need. Make me a voice for your love, truth, mercy, and grace for the cause and lives of the oppressed, the wounded, and the unborn.

Lord, may I walk, stand, and sit humbly in your counsel. Open my ears and let me hear, that I may proclaim your words and the Word to your people and all who you want to draw near. You, Lord, are a God nearby and a God far away. In Jesus's name I pray, my Lord and my Righteousness. Amen. (Jeremiah 23:18, 22, 28; I Kings 22:19; Psalm 1:1; Psalm 118:24 ESV)

I shared part of my story with my sister. How glad we were that I had not divorced Bob after that family vacation in Door County. We would not have John. We both almost stopped breathing at the thought of it. The kids alone made my suffering worthwhile, worth the prices paid. The Three were born out of the love of God.

10

ME AND MY SHADOW

LONELINESS, AN
UNWELCOME GUEST

Katy encouraged me to pray through my visits to the places of my past. In fact, all of my children advised with great wisdom and compassion that I put my concealed carry permit to use. As I went undercover to visit these places of the past, I carried my Bible concealed in my purse and ready-to-load prayer ammunition in my pocket.

My trek back in time took me to our first home, a one-bedroom apartment on Miller Place. Once a very dark shade of evergreen, it was now painted yellow. I recognized the now-yellow metal post across the street from the driveway. Yes, that was the post I backed into one day. The smell of hops from the Miller Brewery, just doors away, would rush in as I exited the back door. It was a reliable trigger for morning sickness, soon to be complemented by the smell of dish soap, coffee, and griddle grease as I got to my Pancake House job at 6:00 a.m. The living room floor had a sort of slope to it, like a multidepth swimming pool. It featured one closet and one bathroom. No shower. All this for thirty-five dollars in rent per month. Oh, yes, and the neighbor's maniacal dog that barked viciously whether you were coming or going (or just standing) was just fine once you realized you would not be torn limb from limb.

One early morning at the restaurant, when the fragrance of dish soap mixed with early morning brew set off my twenty-four-hour "morning" sickness, I let myself run to the bathroom and throw up. I realized right away I couldn't do that again. Once I started, I couldn't stop. So whenever nausea was getting the best of me, I would just swallow ten or twelve times—small swallows that I thought were unnoticeable—while I took someone's order or rang up the bill. Having two poached eggs on dry toast just about every day was nicely doable, healthy for the baby and antinausea-friendly for me. Cheese blintzes were also quite yummy for the both of us.

As I now sat in my parked car outside the yellow duplex, a cloud of heaviness was detectable. It hovered, lingered, and remained. I was sad; I was alone. I said to myself and then wrote in my journal:

It was here at Miller Place that loneliness became an unwelcome guest.

I went on to write out a prayer as I paused there on the side of the road: *Forgive me, Lord, and thank you for sustaining me in this adversity. Thank you for watching over me. Help me to let go and release any hold this place has on me. Help me to forgive.*

In this place, I had been nineteen, pregnant, and alone. I had talked to no one about this nineteen-year-old Mary. Here, I knew I was not pretty and certainly not precious to my husband, for he was abandoning me. I was so alone. I was so sad. Visualizing the rooms inside, I could see the large, velvety, burgundy floral couch and dull green chair or love seat we had gotten from St. Vincent DePaul for fifty dollars. A large, colorful print of a lion and one of a tiger were hung above the furniture. When we were out and about, Bob had picked out the lion picture; I told him we couldn't afford to buy it. He wasn't particularly happy about that and seemed upset and distant. I was afraid of still more rejection and wanted to please him. While he was at classes, I bought the lion and then the tiger picture, too. He had hung a large picture of Robert Kennedy on the dining room wall, I think it was. In the "back to where I came from" reflections, I remembered my father saying that the place did not look like my place. It all spoke of Bob. "Mary" wasn't anywhere to be found.

Forgive me for disobeying my parents and dishonoring them in any way. Forgive me for abandoning what you had drawn me to. Thank you for being an overcoming God.

LONELINESS MOVES IN

Our next home was a second-floor apartment in another suburb. An Old English sheepdog lived next door. He was a sweet dog. In winter, he would go outside and lie contentedly on the ice-covered walkway. My new neighbor would cut my hair and we would talk. One of my lifelines when I lived there was my German Bible, *Die Heilige Schrift*. I landed on Psalm 139 and it became a chapter that I read over and over again. It brought me peace and helped me to feel loved and cared about, cared for. It is hard to believe that in time, I threw that very same Bible in the garbage while I lived in this second home of ours. This place was where my loneliness was horrible. Here, loneliness took up residence. (Psalm 139: 1-18 is recorded in the Notes following the Epilogue.)

My husband bought and raced a go-kart and we also went to a lot of car races. I prayed that God would protect the baby from the endless, loud noise. To think now that I thought then that if we could only afford some pretty clothes for me and some fancy shoes, I would be prettier so he would not need anyone else.

Always his decisions. Always his desires. I supported and defended him at every turn. I remember being so tired when I lived here. We lived in this place a long time. It seems like a lifetime. Three different times when I was home alone in the evening, I took a nice, warm bath. I leaned back to rest awhile and fell asleep for three-plus hours. (Ooh, the water was chilly by then. I haven't taken a bath since. Showers!)

A beige-and-black beaded bamboo curtain hung between the small kitchen and living room. A very sweet memory was giving my little Joy a bath in her little, white plastic tub placed on the kitchen table. I could make the area nice and cozy. Her black hair sprang into tight curls when it was wet. I can see her now, so adorable. We took long walks together and read stories for over an hour before bedtime and before naps when I was home. Katy was born here. I remember when I came home from the hospital with Katy. As we entered the apartment where little Joy was waiting with Grandma, I can remember sweet Joy saying, "Oh, my baby, my baby!" In God's grace I could so enjoy my children and have fun with them. Of them, many happy memories rush in.

I made a photo album of my Joy for Bob; later I made another one of Katy. I pasted in pictures of her as she grew and notes about the cute things she did and said. I wrote about her favorite books and toys and foods when she was so tiny. I remember it was here that I threw out my old albums of pictures Mom and Dad had given me of me growing up and an album of pictures I took as a kid on family vacations. I was making albums of my children and throwing out my own.

Sometimes crazy memories broke in as I pondered these past self-defining experiences that were refusing to be ignored anymore: I was washing my first baby's cloth diapers; the first disposables way back then were very perfumy and irritating for her. As I first selected a cycle to rinse the ripe, soaked, and stained diapers first before washing them, my husband said it was stupid and refused to let me do it. I tried to stand my ground. I was trying everything that might help to keep her rash free and comfy. I grabbed the dial and set it for rinse. He turned the dial off. I wasn't permitted to decide and do even this one little thing. He was intimidating and bigger than me, so I gave up. I gave in. I felt alone.

One day when I was home alone, I pounded our old, hardwood coffee table with a Farberware frying pan. The frying pan ended up a bit dented; the coffee table a bit rougher. Take note that Farberware is exceptionally tough stuff. I guess you could say that the pan was more than a bit dented—but still usable, as was the coffee table. The apartment was a very sad and oppressive place for me. If a particular event triggered this outburst of anger, I could not tell you which it was. I believe this energy surge was an eruption of emotional gases building up in the quagmire of injuries and wounding I tolerated and the rejection and betrayal I denied.

I drove to the parking lot behind the apartment. There *were* many happy times. I could tell you of so many. I recalled my daughter's first birthday party with all of the family there. I remembered when I hollered from the back porch that I was pregnant with my second daughter. I would recognize Bob's footsteps and the rattle of his keys when he came home from work, and I would be glad. Once when we lived in our house, my second daughter drew a picture of Bob and me. In conversation bubbles above the figures representing us, she had written, "I love you, Bob." And in the other, "I love you, Mary." The children did, in fact, see love in there. I loved my husband. I loved him unconditionally and undeniably. I really thought that he loved me all those years. But I think now: how could he have?

One day, I walked with my little one to the corner bakery. I had a bit of change. I asked the woman at the counter how much two donuts would cost. I recounted the small change in my hand. My Joy was looking at all the fancy donuts. A woman standing next to me asked me if she could buy my daughter a very cute, special Easter donut. "Yes, and thank you very much." I explained to my daughter that the woman had bought it for her. We walked home.

Another day, we walked to the opposite corner. There was a very yummy Italian restaurant there. Just a bit earlier, I had searched for and found my dark blue cardboard coin collection folder and pushed out all the Buffalo nickels I had saved when I was a kid. I figured I had enough to buy one of their super lasagna dinners for my husband. I did just that, and my little daughter and I took it to him at work.

Yes, there were many happy times and time spent with my adorable daughter was delightful. But this apartment, this place, was one of the most upsetting and unspeakable places of my life. It was an awful, lonely, sad, dark time in my life. And it was the place where I threw out the Bible.

One night, I was in a very dark place. I had gone to bed with my husband. We had enjoyed each other. Then I touched his back ever so lightly with my fingertips and traced his back up and down and back and forth. I would hold my left arm with my right hand so I could keep my touch very light, faint almost. That's what he liked; that's how he liked it. He fell asleep; I could not.

Troubled thoughts began to shroud my mind like a thickening blanket of smoke. I went out into the living room and sat down on the couch. I had made love with my husband, but I was so very alone. After a while, I laid down on my back with the back of my head resting on the arm of the couch. I was alone. I was sad.

Now, I would say that I was depressed. I don't remember a particular incident that triggered this moment. I believe it was a growing sense of despair, and that I was slipping deeper and deeper into this dark place. Still unable to sleep, I found myself staring at the wooden crucifix that hung on the opposite wall. It was a wedding gift. A small, dark shadow slowly edged over the figure of Christ on the cross. The shadow got larger; the shadow got darker. It covered the cross and got larger still. As it grew larger and darker, it moved toward the couch where I was lying and watching. It totally blocked any view of the crucifix and grew thicker, deeper, and closer. It covered the walls. It was right there. It was close to me. I screamed loudly. It was an awful scream. The baby was surely frightened, and she cried out. My husband ran from the bedroom and charged out to the living room and then the baby cried again. He didn't know where to run. I was screaming and he couldn't get to me. He said to me later it was as if he had run into a giant wall of water. It was stopping him, holding him back. Then the shadow went away, more quickly than it had formed. I don't remember ever feeling so frightened.

While all these reruns of my life in this second home were reeling through my mind as I continued on the downward climb into my past, I found my heart spinning in the melancholy memories. I wrote a prayer in my journal. *What did you want me to do, God? How was I supposed to find you in my despair? How was I supposed to know you were there? Tell me! What should I have done?*

Later I wrote, *Why does Bob show no remorse? Is his heart hardened? Then break it! Soften it! Shake him and wake him to this awfulness! God, what happened to me? Thank you for not letting Satan get inside my soul. Thank you for my scream. I am sorry I threw out your Word. Why and when did I do that, God? I am sorry I hurt you, God. I am sorry.*

When I lived in this apartment, there were those nights when Bob would come home especially late from second shift at the hospital and say he had stopped to help people who were in a car accident on the freeway. I tried to believe him, but my denial didn't hold. The way he told me gave him away. It made no sense, that many accidents on his way home. I knew he had been with Rita. Why did I love Bob? The evidence says it made no difference to him. He cheated on me multiple times. He did not protect me or defend me, but sat aside without intervening as I experienced shame, embarrassment, and confusion. He did not mention me in his news article. He betrayed me time and time again. He hurt me time and time again. He never recognized or thanked me for what I did to support him, for the sacrifices I made. He refused to say he was sorry.

As I recalled and wrote these stories of my past, my inner voice now shouted in my soul: *I will be valued. I will be loved. I will be appreciated. I will not tolerate being betrayed, lied to. I will not give up or sacrifice friends, dreams, family or faith. I was alone. No one knew. My husband did not care.*

Later, as I sat in my car, staring at the old apartment building and recalling the past, I prayed, *Father, where were you? Thank you for keeping me alive, for allowing me to eat healthy and pray for Joy and Katy. Thank you for sparing my life. Forgive me that in ignorance, sin, and blindness, I did not hear you or see you; yet you helped me to survive. Change me, Lord! Lead me out of this quagmire and through this dark wall into your safekeeping, into your love and truth. Give me endurance to serve only you all the days of my life! Help me to overcome and release these memories if that is what I must do. Use this now, Lord, so we can be done with it and that I might live loudly and fully in you! In Jesus's name I pray. Amen."*

I had brought my new German Bible with me when I visited the second apartment, the second home. As I sat in the car, I read Psalm 139. I whispered, *Lord, forgive me. I thank you for loving me.* Then I prayed through Psalm 139.

One night, when we lived in the flat, our third home before John was born, Joy and Katy were in bed and I was sewing a dress for Katy. The fabric had small white and pink squares, and I was making the finishing touches. I was very excited to show it to Bob when he got home from working at the hospital late that night. I had taken a popular "Stretch and Sew" class with my mother-in-law and was having fun sewing things. It was the first time I could actually sew things and they turned out. Ha! I even made my husband a jumpsuit for the race track. I sewed bike jerseys for the both of us. (I remember now that when Joy wasn't even born yet, I had started to make a little white t-shirt for her with a gold band and a black band along the neckline and sleeves. It was a surprise for her daddy, for it would match her daddy's softball uniform.)

As I was finishing the cute pink- and-white dress for our adorable Katy, I said to myself, "Bob isn't coming home tonight. He won't be here. Why am I so eager to finish this? He's not going to make it home." It was a very strong and very sure feeling. Anxiousness set in and grew as it got later and later.

The phone rang. It was my mother-in-law. Bob had been hit by some young people who were drag racing and ran a stop sign. He was thrown into the corner of the windshield and had sustained a severe neck injury. I went to the hospital. The next day, when I went back to the hospital with the girls, little Katy wore her new pink-and-white dress. Her daddy was wearing a neck brace and had to keep his head and neck motionless. Little Katy lay down on his chest and put her arms around him and hugged him, held him. I can still see it now. It was precious.

So, what was it like to look back at the suppression, shame, and sadness; the abuse, abandonment, and aloneness; the humiliation and betrayal?

I could not go back there without Beth to guide the process or without the faithfulness and support of family and friends. I could not look back upon it without the nearness of God. As I felt the pain of the past, I was moved to consider the suffering of Christ, his suffering for me. Jesus was completely alone, abandoned by even God.

Lord, you have prepared me for this downward climb. You have made me stronger, and you are with me as I search out and walk through the buried past. I claim your wisdom and new learning as I work my way through these many memories, as I study your Word, and as I read other books you make available to me. Protect me and help me as I share my stories with family, friends, and my climbing guide. I am blessed, for you are my God. I am blessed with this opportunity to go deep into my past and search out the learning you want me to know. Thank you for Joy, Katy, and John and all they bring to my life and living. Thank you for Jerry and Jan, Mom and Dad. Search me, stretch me, use me, and lead me. Shape me and prepare me for whatever you desire me to be for your kingdom purposes. Keep me gentle and humble in heart. I love you, God. I want to now and forever more love you with all my heart, mind, body, and soul. Help me to do this. Bless my entire family and be with my other friends. Bring those who do not know you into a saving relationship with Jesus Christ. I pray this in your name and by your grace. Amen.

As I worked through this phase to the other side of the wall where there would be the most freedom, most clarity, and most wisdom to choose; I felt self-understanding and awareness unfold, along with a clearer knowing of Christ.

My climbing guide clarified that Bob had offered me the special position of being his wife, a permanent and important role. I would be the one he always came back to. She said, "He needed you. You were in bondage to his life and assumed into his identity. Serving that hope of him not rejecting you, serving that hope of him loving you, serving this idea, became your idol and you poured your tenacity and stubbornness into the effort. You are very tenacious, steadfast, determined, and resolute."

He could not love me the way I wanted to be loved. He was not with me when I needed him. While he was out with other women, I was alone.

In his divine sovereignty, God allowed all of the pain of the past and used it for good.

Lord, may I never disregard your sacrifice or betray your love. I choose to live my life loving you. I desire an exuberant, true, intimate, and devoted relationship with you. Free me from pride and don't let me even come close to any unhealthy, idolatrous attachments. Help me to be certain and confident of who I am in your love. And Lord, please show me: Why did I let go of the dreams you had given me? The opportunities we had worked toward? In Jesus's name I pray. Amen.

In some of the books I read, an affair was referred to as shattering and catastrophic. It was helpful for me to read that description. As someone who had denied her own pain and anguish, such a statement told me, "Yes, this is something that would hurt like hell. It is okay for you to hurt." So, deep anguish and sadness must be okay, then.

DID YOU EVER SIT WITH YOUR LONELINESS?

My good friend Dr. Beth asked me, "Mary, did you ever sit with your loneliness?"

I took in the question. *Did I ever sit with my loneliness?* I didn't answer for some time. In the long pause, I couldn't name a time that I had sat down with my loneliness.

What does loneliness look like, after all? Have I known loneliness? Did I at some time sit down with loneliness, or did I send loneliness away, not letting it stay? Surely I did not welcome it in for a visit. Working harder, working longer, lifting weights and getting stronger, running distances, biking more, all that was a race away from loneliness? Did I study late and eat Oreos and M&Ms to coat it with a confectionery blend? Did I sip the drink of fermented grapes to please my palate and contain the stain of being without another so as not to feel it just then?

But if a life experience and emotional mix creates this thing called loneliness and you are in that place, how can you send it away? It doesn't have legs to move on and go elsewhere. A cover placed over it just keeps it under. It keeps it undercover, under wraps, under the radar, but still there.

Did I see the shadow of loneliness in my rearview mirror? Did I see it in a side glance, or was it over my head? Did I close my eyes and laugh louder so as not to sense the unwelcome presence of loneliness? So what did (or does) loneliness look like? Do I know it when I feel it, or do I consider it some unknown phantom? When I stood before a mirror, was that loneliness I saw with me in my reflection, separate from myself? As I reflected on the notion of a looming presence staring blankly at my mirrored person, did I detect a defect, see a flaw, a failing, an imperfection that would cause me to be disregarded and rejected or not even considered? Did I perceive something spoiled, something sad, and something branded with shame?

Was loneliness always here, these many years, seated beside me in the "long-term consequences of betrayal?"

Did I ever sit with my loneliness? What does loneliness look like?

TEACHINGS ON LONELINESS

At the beginning of my session with Dr. Beth on January 2nd, I quickly shared how grand my Christmas had been. As I drove to my daughter's and son-in-law's home to join my kids and grandknuckleheads for a Christmas brunch, I was actually laughing and smiling in the car. It truly was a splendid time with my children and grandchildren, followed by a very fun time with extended family. I love getting together with my brother and sister and their families. Family gatherings, for me, were a time to look forward to. With or without caffeine, I would be supercharged in anticipation of sharing time and creating new memories with family. This was going to be good—great!

Beth asked me, "What is it that you need that your children can't give you?" I was stumped, actually. The Six were my best friends. They make me laugh. I love them all to pieces. I enjoy their persons and their personalities. They know me. They love me. They are honest with me. They encourage me. I like to be with them and they like to be with me. They couldn't be any finer. We talk together, walk together, travel together, run together, bike together, swim together, camp together, eat together, and sleep in tents together in the great Northwoods of Wisconsin. We share the fun the sad the good the bad the scared the strong the short the long the ins and outs the cheers the doubts, the hopes the flops the dreams—what *don't* we share?

I later realized, "Wait a minute, that isn't the point of the question." My kids are all I could imagine them to be, and then some. I was looking for something in the realm of what they *can* give me, and they give it all. *The question is: what do I need that they* can't *give me?* I had bolted around the question. I had put the brakes on in my thinking. What do I need that they *can't* give me?

This time, my response was not delayed: An intimate relationship. A husband to love and hold me, a husband for me to love and hold. Ah. So that is the seed of my loneliness…

I recalled the message of a missionary at church the other week. I actually cannot remember the point he was making, but he asked all the married couples to stand and give each other a hug, even if they had had a bad start to the day. Then he asked the children to stand up and join them. As the invitations to stand went on, the singles were never included. We sat there among the hundreds of others still standing. We were not drawn in. We were left out. We remained seated. It was crummy…no, *lousy*. Or lonely?

Beth commented, "It seems you feel that to express loneliness makes you appear ungrateful."

I told her that I had told a friend I was dating again and wanted to find a "rest-of-my-life" companion. I wanted to be married. The response from him was, "You have such beautiful kids. They are amazing." And I thought, "Don't you think I know that? Do you think I am ungrateful?" My friend was someone who I know would be happy beyond measure if I did find such a companion. I was inferring that he was implying I was not counting my blessings.

Beth said, "The faith element is often spoken of in regard to loneliness: 'If you have an intimate relationship with God, and know you are always in his presence, you cannot be lonely.' However, intimacy with God is not a substitute for intimacy with human beings. Religion may say you should not be lonely. 'You should be completely satisfied with God.' With a desire to do the *right thing*, Christians often deny their loneliness. But if God designed us to be solely satisfied with him, why would he have created us and put us here with other human beings?"

Later in the session Beth added, "One of the hardest aspects of betrayal is loneliness, and you bore up to it. People are often ashamed to express that they are lonely. They think, 'I am alone. I am alone, so I am lonely. I am lonely because I am defective.' It is a profound loneliness. You need to feel it. Not cover over it. You need to remember what it was like."

I interjected, "Remember when we had acted out the meeting with Young Mary and Now Mary, Now Mary had asked what it was like to be Young Mary. I had said *I feel so alone.*"

Beth had said, "Who was asking whom?"

Ah! Yes, I said. It could have been the Now Mary asking the Young Mary *or* the Young Mary asking the Now Mary. The answer could be the same: "I feel so alone." The young Mary's response was rising from a deep, wounded loneliness that was desperate and awful and severe. The Now Mary also knows loneliness. I still resist sitting with it.

Beth shared, "Loneliness can be a long-term consequence of betrayal when a spouse is not partnering up or in circumstances that are overwhelming. You can be lonely even in a relationship."

Beth continued. *You hide loneliness from your family. Sometimes, maybe, you are extra cheerful. You don't want them to see it, to feel it. You don't have to work so hard to cover. Don't be a sad sap or be extra cheerful, but be an authentic middle of the road. You—we—shun the loneliness part. It comes behind you like a shadow. You shush it away if it shows up. Make sure all parts of you are welcome. Your cheerfulness is truly your gift to the world. You light up a room. When your ex is in the room, it accentuates your loneliness. You accommodate the discomfort and act invisible.*

During the session, Beth said, "It must have been difficult for you to go to events with Bob and Joan there."

I started to cry as soon as she completed her sentence. "Thank you." You see, Beth heard my story, watched my face, and listened for my heart. Yes, it was difficult. It still is I guess. I still feel the same. Now I have the name for it and someone understands. I can start to deal with it. (And now after completing this manuscript and editing it once again, I recognize how hard and exhausting it was and is. I really hate it; I am so tired of it. This year as I was finishing this manuscript, there was a new injury. I just don't want to be where Bob and Joan are. I don't want to deal with it all.)

Included, yet part of me excluded. "To protect your children, you did not show your loneliness." I nodded yes. She was right.

I recalled the time when I was sitting in the bleachers of the pool deck between my daughter's races and talking with some other parents. I looked up. My separated husband and Joan were outside the large pool windows across the way, in full view of everyone. She was leaning against the outside brick wall of the school and he faced her, leaning in with his hands placed on the bricks on either side of her. They were both laughing. I didn't say anything. I just got up and walked down the bleachers and off the pool deck. I was sad. I felt shame. I was alone.

Later, I remembered planning to go to a dinner gathering at my friend Cindy's house a short time after the divorce. I was feeling sad, but I went anyway. I was quiet. Cindy noticed, so I told her I was feeling sad and kind of down. She said, "I am glad you came over anyway." That was a rare moment for me, and Cindy's gentle acceptance was nice. I am genuinely a cheerful and very happy person. It's who I am. But the loneliness, the sad, I, well…I guess I do keep it under wraps.

I remembered my son and others being so surprised when I shared with them that I wanted to date again. I think I was surprised too. Loneliness had been an unrecognized companion for a long time.

OFF-ROAD—AND WHAT A RIDE!

On Friday morning, January 6, 2012, in a quiet moment I remembered another time I had tried to hold back loneliness. It was in the fall of 1997, a day after Joy's wedding and the day Katy was off to Barbados and Guyana for six months with Youth with a Mission. The wedding was wonderful. Joy was beginning a new life with her new husband. I loved and love them both dearly. I, too, was moving on in my journey. I was sending one daughter off on a marriage adventure, and another on an international mission adventure.

Before I headed to the airport to say good-bye to Katy, I loaded my off-road bike into the car, grabbed my helmet, bike shoes, and gloves. I filled a few water bottles and snatched some energy bars from the cupboard. My Bible was already in the car. Katy was going to the airport with her dad and Joan. After arriving at Mitchell Airport, I sat down in the chairs by the boarding area. It was before 9/11, when you could still say good-bye to your friends and family right at the gate, minutes before they boarded the plane. I sat in a chair across from a number of people, including two women about my age who were talking with each other. The three of us joined in conversation.

They were going to be boarding the same plane as my daughter. I shared with the two women how I was saying good-bye to my daughter as she headed out on a mission trip to Barbados and told them that her dad and his wife should be arriving with her soon. I was worried that I would not have the chance to hug her and hold her before she boarded the plane. (I am sitting with my loneliness right now at my computer as I go back to these memory "snapshots." I am learning to recognize loneliness and sadness and allow its presence.) The two women listened with caring attentiveness.

My daughter, my ex-husband, and his wife Joan arrived. My ex-husband hugged my daughter and then Joan did, for a long time. I wanted to hug her, too. I wanted to hold her. Time was running short. People were boarding. I rubbed Katy's back. Joan pulled her away and then spun her away from me. The two women had risen from their chairs and had walked over to me. I looked up. The care and understanding I perceived in their faces was a comfort to me. They looked at me with what seemed to me a sincere intent to let me know they understood. I had left my purse at my seat across from them. They had picked it up as they prepared to board and set it by me as I stood there by my daughter. I later wrote in my Bible, "God sent two angels to the airport so that I would not be alone. How marvelous he was to do that." My daughter actually said she never noticed them on the plane. Whether angels or not, I am confident God used their presence to help me in that moment of loneliness. So, I didn't feel completely alone.

At last I got to hug Katy and tell her how I loved her. I was sad that this circumstance and its dynamics were surely hard for her to bear. My manner of living through these encounters was typically (depending on the situation) to push away my feelings or choose not to insert myself in order to protect my children.

I headed to my car in the airport lot and got onto the freeway. As I drove to the Northern Kettle Moraine to ride the Greenbush off-road trails, I cried. I cried harder than I ever had, all the way for the hour-plus drive. My tears were streaming down my face and beginning to affect my visibility. I thought I should pull off the freeway. The flooding tears were like the opening of a man-made dam on a strong and beautiful river that had held it back unnaturally for a long time, at last releasing the waters to let the river flow as it should, freely, in strength and power, wherever it was intended to go.

I arrived at the trailhead. As I prayed in the car, I heard God's instructions to take all of this heavy heart baggage, pack it in an imaginary backpack, and lay the heavy pack down before I rode the trails. I took the newly awakened emotional pressure that had burst the dam and shoved it into "the pack." I moved through the motions of actually placing it on the grass in front of the parked car. No one else was there. I was alone at the trailhead.

I rode every trail of the Greenbush area several times. I rode hard. I cranked hard down the hills and up the hills. I did not brake or hesitate. I was flying. It was one of the finest off-road rides I ever had. I pushed it for twenty-nine miles. And all the while, Jesus was right beside me. Who would have thought that Jesus was a mountain biker? How sweet is that?

I rode back to the parking lot and leaned my bike up against the car. I loosened my helmet and switched out my shoes. I paused to say thanks for a great ride and then put my bike in the car. After driving to the Long Lake area of the Northern Kettles, I parked the car and grabbed a pack with my Bible, a pen, and a water bottle.

As I closed the car, locked the doors, and headed toward the shore of the lake, my heart joined my mind that had just returned to the loaded backpack set down at the trailhead. As I walked, I realized full well that no one else can ever really understand our grief, our pain, our sorrow. No one really knows me on the inside. No one knows how this all affects me, who I am and how I am with all I have personally lived, experienced, and known and how it interacts with the unique person that is me. No one knows my story.

Friends and family love and care deeply, but can never fully know. My children love me. They love me so very much. The Three will never know the story. They can't understand this. No one understands. No one knows. No one knows, for I have not shown them. I have not told them.

Jesus came up alongside me and said, "*I understand, and I am here.*"

119

Imagine that you are walking and someone joins you. You do a quick step to adjust your gate so you can walk in rhythm. That is what I did just then. Jesus placed his arm around my shoulders, and I did a quick step so we were in walking rhythm. We walked together to the shoreline beyond the main beach area and sat down together on a picnic table bench facing the water.

We sat together there by the Lake. I sat with my loneliness, and Jesus sat with me. I was not alone. Realizing I had left my journal at home, I wrote in the open pages in the front of my Bible: *Jesus said, "I understand. I care and I love you."*

As I opened the pages of my Bible to read Psalm 145:17–21, Psalm 147:1–11, and Psalm 103:1–14, I felt Jesus there next to me on the picnic bench. Jesus knows what I am made of; he knows my heart. I did not desire to hurt others, to injure, or to be angry. I just hurt. I felt his compassion. He just sat with me and showed his love to me. He knew I hurt, even though I had been holding the hurt deep inside myself.

"I don't want to give this burden to you, Jesus. You have carried so much for me already."

"I am here to carry it all. It's all right. I love you."

"You have done so much for me already."

"Give me even this," he said. "This is what I came for."

As I look back to this scene, it stands out as a picture of the palliative care of Jesus. He was comforting and reassuring. He was present. His knowing and understanding, his love, and his grace acted as an immediate and lasting balm for my loneliness. It was powerful. He bore the weight that was crushing me on his shoulders.

Jesus comes alongside us. We are encouraged to go to him as a method for dealing with loneliness. And to be sure, knowing that he's there, that he understands and that he cares is what we need. It is what I needed. And now, after more years have gone by, I have learned that in his great and sovereign plan, God has more to his method of healing us. Just as Jesus made himself known to his friends and asked them to be with him during his trials in the Garden of Gethsemane, we too must make all of ourselves known to at least one human other. In the assurance of his unconditional and extravagant love, in the comfort of his understanding and care, and in the warmth of his embrace, he makes it safe for us to let ourselves be known to others. Being known and still loved by God and being known and still loved by others diminishes loneliness, for the dammed-up emotions are released and lose their power. Freedom flows.

RECOLLECTIONS OF LONELINESS

When I remained in my relationship with my husband for so many years, I continuously denied myself. I devalued myself by staying in the relationship. I saw myself investing more and more of myself in the relationship as I hung on and hung in, giving up more and more of me. As I went through separation, divorce, and the aftermath, I would consider how I once thought that my giving up of self again and again made the relationship priceless. But I see now and must acknowledge that my husband did not care. It was of no value to him. He still would not remain by my side or support me. He would not say, "Mary was always there for me." I devalued myself by staying and not giving up. Ironically, what I gave up was invested in a relationship with someone who did not care. I feel as if I cheated myself out of my years of young love. I will never have that back.

Having and raising my children was delightful. There is nothing I would change there. And I had a wonderful childhood. There are so many who lose their childhoods in abuse and neglect. That is so very sad. I know I have so much to be grateful for. God has blessed me richly. But I can't have my years of young love back. I will grieve my loss of young love, and I am finally acknowledging my loneliness all these years. So is this, then, the bottom of the crevasse?

For many years after my divorce, while my children and I still lived in the house all five of us had lived in as a family, I kept my road bike in my bedroom. One day, when my mother and father were over for a visit, I said to my mother, "Kinda crazy, I suppose, that I keep my bike in my bedroom."

"It makes you happy. It's good for you to have it there."

My ex would pick up the kids and as they headed out to his car, I would lean my back against the heavy, wooden front door and slide down the door to the floor. I would sit there for a while. I felt numb. After a time, I would go to my bedroom, pack my gym bag, and head to the YMCA to work out. Eventually, I would have my gym bag ready to go so I didn't have time to think of the sad and loneliness. I headed to the YMCA to lift and to run.

On July 4th that year, a holiday and my young son's birthday, I was home alone. So I packed my gym bag and went to work out. After my workout, I remember the branch executive seeing me as I headed out the front exit. He said to the reception staff at the desk, "See, I told you we should be open on the 4th." At the time, he didn't know who I was.

As I said, "Yes. I am sure glad you were open today," I was thinking, "You have no idea just how good it was that you were open. Things might have turned out differently." I had finished my workout and my cloud of desperate feelings had passed over.

For all those years of shared custody, I would draw a smiley face on the Saturday of the week the kids would be with me and a sad face on the weeks they would not be with me. This was a different loneliness, a great and deep missing of them.

Then there were the Christmas Eves, with all the family and hubbub, and then my children going to their dad's home at 9:00 p.m. and me going home alone. A few times I stayed overnight at my sister's home. That was always lovely, and I know I was always welcome to stay.

One week when the kids were with their dad, Katy had left one of her high-tops on the living room floor, tipped on its side and laces flopped over. I left it there, for it seemed more like the kids were around. It made me think of them; I would smile and feel happy. John's squirt gun was on the living room chair. Two pairs of muddy handprints were on the garage wall next to the child-hand-painted grey-blue dolphin by the door into the house. There they stayed, even when I sold the house.

As I reviewed my journal records of my visits to the four places I had lived with my husband, I noted how so many times, I described myself as so very lonely in the different scenes I recalled. I remember thinking years ago that the loneliness after my divorce was not as awful as the loneliness I knew when I was married. And that loneliness was still present and buried deep within a yet-uncharted crevasse.

Later, as I wrote again in my journal, I recalled my unexpected return to the sadness and loneliness of my more recent past on the bleachers at my granddaughter's basketball game. It was so much fun to watch her. My daughter and her husband were there. Her half-brother and his wife and my ex-husband and his wife were there. I looked at the moms and dads on the bleachers in front of me, husbands and wives watching their kids. There were couples all around me. The group of three couples and my two granddaughters were going out for lunch together after the game. I said good-bye before they all left, and I headed out to the parking lot. I actually had my gym bag packed to go to the YMCA, wouldn't you know! That's when I got the call from the Bob #2 who rejected me.

When I saw my ex-husband's and Joan's son together with his wife when she was pregnant, the young man (my ex-husband's son) was so tender to his pregnant wife and touched her tummy. I was happy for them. Yet sadness was undeniably there for me. I had been very lonely when I was so young and pregnant for the first time.

Yes, God does indeed fill that God-shaped hole in my heart. He is ever near, ever present. He resides within me. But the company of a husband, I have not known. I have not let myself be known. In these regards, I have been forever lonely.

Loneliness had been the camouflaged companion, always there walking alongside, but kept at arm's length.

JUST HOW CAN I BE LONELY? AFTER ALL, I AM LIVING WITH THREE MALES

Two of the males I live with absolutely love me. I am not sure about the third (he does *like* me). The three males are Boaz, my yellow Labrador; Gideon, my cat; and Marty, my cinnamon ball python (but he is just a baby).

Then there are the Eleven. As I mentioned before others have rightly contended, "You know, Mary, you have three beautiful children with three wonderful spouses, and now five grandchildren. They are all amazing." When people say things like this, I assume they are telling me to simply be grateful for what I have. I may be inferring (correctly or incorrectly) from their conversation that I am not grateful or don't realize the many blessings I have. I just want to say to them, "You know me. Do you really think I am ungrateful? And that for the past twenty-eight years I have done nothing but languish and flounder around?"

Gratitude and gladness, joy and great cheerfulness, and thankful recognition of all that I have been given do not go unexpressed in my life. I have had a full and abundant life. My parents are wonderful. I had what I have sometimes called a textbook happy childhood. I love my brother and sister dearly. We were friends growing up together, and we remain treasured friends to one another. I love their spouses and all my nieces and nephews. Under the umbrella of the unmatchable grace of God, I have flourished. God working in my life (even when I had rejected and betrayed him) is the reason I not only survived, but thrived. His mercy endures forever. He has redeemed me, my life, and my dreams in so many ways.

Yet there is loneliness present. It is part of who I am. I did not name it and outright claim it before. I needed to share my story to come to grips with it, identify it, and release the need to push it away to protect myself. It is no longer looming about my reflected self; it is a part of me to be taken in and respectfully regarded. To dwell on it and ruminate about it and lie down with it could trigger depression. To recognize it, sit with it, know it, and share it is crucial. Sometimes we tell ourselves or others, "Just get over it!" Trying to "just get over it" is a futile farce that keeps us stuck in the grip of denial, trapped in the fog of depressed loneliness in some or all areas of our lives, and plants us in the world of make-believe.

I am still without a "rest-of-my-life-on-earth" companion, a handsome husband, the man I desire to love and to hold, to walk and talk with, to snuggle and sleep with, to have sex and have sex with (a double emphasis there), someone to enjoy physically and to be physically enjoyed by (ah, there it is again), someone to know and be known by, someone to share my faith with, to wrestle with emotions and ideas and to share dreams with, someone to encourage and be encouraged by, someone to cry and laugh with, someone to go to church and Bible study with. I can sit right next to him with my arm lying right along his. I can rest my hand on his thigh. When the pastor says to turn and greet one another, I can kiss him on the lips. He would be someone I can have and hold and cherish and likewise be cherished by.

It indeed is God we all need beyond all else and all others. God is our God, our Savior, and our Father who is in heaven and in our being. God is our Redeemer and Friend, our Creator, our Wonderful Counselor. He is full of grace, ever present, and loves us always. He is the Reason we live and breathe and have our being.

A husband would not replace God in my life, and God doesn't replace a lost or nonexistent husband. His love can spill over and soothe the emptiness and loneliness there, but "He" doesn't replace "him." Consider Adam and Eve. God made Adam and knew all along that an Adam needed an Eve, an Eve needed an Adam, and that they both needed God, to walk with him and talk with him and each other in the grand garden.

If I marry again, he will not replace my first love, the father of my children. I once told my son that there was no one else I would want to be his father. But the new husband will touch my life and my living all on his own and be the companion I desire.

Now, this is the thing about God. He is not going away. He died on a cross once and rose again after three days. He is eternal. He is the unmoved mover. He created all there is. No human being, no fabricated false god, no material wealth or item, no success or fame can replace God. There is only one God. He is here forever and nothing can be what he is, do what he does, or fill us up like he can. There is a place in our hearts that is God shaped. No other thing or being can fill it up, no matter how hard we might try. We might as well try to fill in the Grand Canyon with a grain of sand.

God is God. To live without him is awful and to die without him is the worst thing that could ever happen.

God knows and understands that I desire a husband, and he is okay with that. The high and mighty and holy God can't be replaced by a husband. He won't tolerate me trying to replace him with anything. I did that with Bob. I went to a place where I pushed God away; I betrayed God and I forfeited myself. That was not good. It was a hell-bent, lost and lonely, fragile and fallen route.

I can live a full and abundant life without a husband, and I will be content. I cannot live a full and abundant life without my God. I have much to be grateful for, and it is okay that I still desire a husband. I will go on with joy in my life without a husband for a companion, but it could be quite nice to walk the trails with a husband and Boaz. You can be certain that with or without a husband, with or without a Labrador, I will be walking the trail with my God.

So what does dear Webster say about the word *alone?* It is typically used to stress the fact of being by yourself, while *lonely* suggests a longing for companionship. *Lonesome* introduces the element of sadness. *Loneliness* is a state of being sad from being alone and amplifies the sense of sadness, bleakness, and cheerlessness. (Webster, p.703)

Loneliness is also a distasteful residue left behind when you or I forfeit self, suppress feelings, or withdraw. (Beth Johnson)

I recall that when I became engaged to George in 1989, at one moment I said out loud without meaning to: "I'm going to be alone again." It was like a forward shock, a future shock. It was as if I were hit by some numbing ray. No. No. I won't go there again.

11

A PARSNIP ON THE
PINNACLE OF YUCK

On a day in July when I met with Beth, I shared how I felt after telling the story of "the pinnacle of yuck."

She made clear that Bob had sucked out my identity and self-esteem to maintain control (or an illusion of it). He only had stolen an illegitimate power and control. Extracting all of the power, he used my vitality so he could give it out to other women.

It was important to see my victimization and to see Bob as a parasite: as a weaker, parasitic human being. For him to see another woman fed on my loss of self-respect. It was sadistic. He got strength from that. I surrendered my power in high school and yielded free access to myself, and he got off on that power. "He stole your power, so your loss would be his gain." My assignment was to see Bob as a parasite in all these things and to see his jealous control.

We revisited the "pinnacle of yuck"—the shaming scenes of matching shirts for wife and mistress. It was a degrading and humiliating farce that allowed Bob to dominate me more and dictate his wishes. I existed only as an object to serve his needs. When Beth asked me what I would now say to Bob when he said, "We should get one for Rita," she translated my restrained, *Miss Mary Nice-Nice* phrasing (as I describe it) to what

I immediately—and at long last—recognized as the more appropriate answer: *Are you fucking crazy?*

I concluded that Bob was a Parasitic, Arrogant, Selfish, Narcissistic, Ignoble Polygamist: a PARSNIP. He fed off of my vitality and power and strength. *You refused to say you were sorry. You betrayed me. You kept inflicting pain and shaming me.* Why? I don't understand why.

During one of our very first sessions Beth assigned some homework. "Google *narcissistic personality!* Unraveling your story is partly about personality theory. Some of our personalities free us up to be our best selves; some manifest ugly parts."

Wikipedia: The Free Encyclopedia at Wikipedia.org says: "Narcissism is the personality trait of egotism, vanity, conceit or simple selfishness." A sense of entitlement is typically central to narcissistic personalities. The site further explains that narcissism is often marked by indifference to the plights of others, grandiose superficial charm, and bloated sense of self-worth. Lack of remorse or guilt, failure to accept responsibility for their own actions, and an inflated sense of their own abilities are also classic traits. Sexual narcissism is a dysfunction in which sexual exploits are pursued, usually in extramarital affairs, to overcompensate for low self-esteem and an inability to express true intimacy. It is a pattern of behavior that reflects an inflated sense of sexual entitlement.

Bob didn't love me, but rather was suppressing, oppressing, and objectifying me. It was futile of me to think if I was more *this* or more *that*, he would love me and stop hurting me. Thinking about all he did and said, and all these things I shared with Beth—seeing it all, seeing how he treated me, it is all so hideous, disgusting, nauseating, and so poisonous. He exhibited the personality traits of narcissism: egotism, selfishness, a sense of entitlement, and indifference to the plight of others. He was unmoved by my distress, anyway.

Bob was poisonous to my self-esteem, my soul, my spirit, my health, my thinking, my being. I wish I never had to see him again.

There is much that hurts, frustrates, baffles, and confuses me about Bob's arrogance and refusal to acknowledge the pain and anguish or to say he was sorry. He doesn't see. He doesn't understand. He doesn't care. He is not capable of doing the right thing. When I step into it, I see that for me to hope for him to say he is sorry, as I did during my marriage, is like expecting him to be able to fly. Thinking I could do more, be more, say more, explain more, operating on the premise that he even cared, was pointless. He didn't care then; he doesn't care now.

I have learned more about my frailties and failures. God has led me on this journey and has allowed me to grow in authenticity and at the same time know him more. I know that God cares for Bob and will work this all out in conformity with his perfect will. I feel that I am grieving. I still have a tendency to intellectualize around all of this. It is difficult for me to sit still and be present in my grief and loneliness.

Lord, give me a husband who loves you, loves himself, and loves me and the children. Someone who is gentle and humble in heart, and not abusive or arrogant, but tender. It seems so impossible, but all things are possible for you.

Bob didn't love me. He did not comprehend the depth of disgrace, shame, and anguish he caused. Still, even now, he will not talk to me, acknowledge my presence, or say he is sorry. He isn't big enough or strong enough to.

Help me, Jesus. Help me to move through this black wall, the dark night of the soul. Do I need to cry? I am sad that I don't have a husband. Sad about those awful years. Sad that I am fifty-nine and have no husband. Sad about this stupid dating thing. Ugh! Sad for eighteen-year-old Mary. She was so hurt. So alone. So sad. So shamed. I am sad for the loss of young love and of not being loved by a tender and caring man all these years.

The parasite doesn't care, and doesn't know or care about the damage it does. It just sucks and feeds off of you. It can be deadly, but you can take medicine that will rid you of it. The parasite has no compassion for its host. I see it now. I am strong. I was always stronger. I am stronger and growing stronger still.

At this moment in my journaling, I got face-down on the floor. I took shame, abuse, degradation, embarrassment, humiliation, despair, and disgrace and laid it down at the foot of the Cross. I imagined Jesus's pierced feet there, bleeding. The words, "Vindicate me, O God," came to my mind. I think—I felt—that as I pondered the scene, this needed to be said.

To vindicate is saturated with meaning. It implies to set free, set right, and deliver. To avenge, absolve, and exonerate. To confirm and substantiate. Vindicate means to advocate for someone and to plead in favor of someone. It means to provide justification or defense and to protect from attack and maintain a right.

As I reworked these words from my journal notes, I realized that I have been vindicated in many ways. I have been able to understand so many things on this journey. Beth, family, and friends have been so supportive and affirming. Books I have read have affirmed my past. I am the one who is so quick to beat myself up, to judge and condemn myself. I am becoming aware of this detrimental tendency and healing has been possible between such paralyzing personal responses.

Bob and I enjoyed each other—at least it appeared that way. When my husband and I were nineteen and married, we went canoeing on the Wisconsin River. It was noon. The sun was overhead and it was hot. I looked at my husband, and he looked at me. "Hmm," I said. "Hmmm," he responded. Then we enjoyed each other. Of course, we had to restrain ourselves a bit or we would have tipped that puppy.

Whenever my husband went to bed, I stopped whatever I was doing and joined him there. I wanted to be with him. We made love. I loved and enjoyed each and every part of him. I loved my husband. My interest remained throughout our marriage, even when I knew he was having an affair, when he was sharing himself with someone else. I never let myself take in the full reality of my husband sharing himself with another, not until now. I see my denial now. (As I wrote this, I felt it. I felt the anguish, because I let myself picture him physically loving another, caring for someone else.)

I had wanted to have sex with my husband; we had sex regularly. (You may ask, "What is your definition of *regularly*?" Ten, twenty times a day. In as many positions. Ha! That is the only statement in this book that isn't quite true.) I know he enjoyed it and wanted to be with me. So why did he need someone else? Why couldn't I be enough? I had said, you know, he would go and spend money when we had just discussed what little we had. After a time, Beth said, "I want you to repeat these things: Bob loved me, but he placed no restrictions on his appetite." This is a defining feature of narcissism: entitlement, no matter what price it was to me or the children.

At one point, Beth asked me to repeat the following as if I were saying it to Bob: (I remember stumbling on the part *I know you love me*. At this point in my life I knew it was not true.) *I know you love me, but you are with another woman, so you can't.* (This was my area of confusion.) *I know you love me, so when will you choose only me?*

Beth said, "His answer, *I won't.*" She added, "You need to think this through. Think about it then, not to be confused. Tell Bob, *You can't choose only me, because you won't say no to yourself.*"

"Let's be very clear. You carried it as rejection when it was not. He claimed it was not a requirement for him to be faithful even before you were married. So let's be clear: It was not rejection. He was running from self. It was a way to distract himself from the human void. His appetite for attention and things and having affairs was an attempt to fill the void in himself. He shifted his pain to you. He never bore his own pain."

"You took it as rejection. It was his greed and a way to distract himself and his inability to be still with self. You carried it as rejection. You were a casualty of a very greedy man. You were not inadequate. You picked up the burden of self-doubt that didn't belong there. Women often reduce self-esteem to deal with the multiple wives thing. Men can't do that."

And often society just doesn't expect them to.

My husband and I were still loving toward each other. My husband continued to sleep with me and we enjoyed each other's company.

Beth added, "I believe Bob regrets the loss of you. He is too proud and arrogant to acknowledge this, but no other woman can compare with you. He lost an incredible woman. He was too greedy, too arrogant. And he lost you. You are not a dime-a-dozen woman. He lost someone pretty amazing. Bob can never say he did not know love. He knew Mary. You are okay with the void. You are very strong. God fills you up and you are okay."

There are certain actions and/or comments that can trigger an unexpected response of depression and sadness in me. I remembered again how, when I asked Beth if she thought I could ever have a healthy relationship with a man, she answered yes. "You are a very strong woman."

I would like a husband. I would like a husband to hold me. But I am strong in God. I am okay.

12

THE SPIRIT MOVING OVER THE DARKNESS OF THE DEEP

DO YOU THINK GOD IS JUST A FAIRY-TALE?

In the beginning God created the heavens and the earth. Now the earth was formless and empty, darkness was over the surface of the deep, and the Spirit of God was hovering over the waters. (Genesis I: 1-2 NIV)

This is a riveting scene to imagine. It is captivating to ponder the Spirit of God moving over the dark and the deep in such an unmatchable moment. The power of the Spirit moving over the darkness in the deep of the human heart is even more astounding.

In divine wisdom, with abundant grace, and through endless love; God will receive the tears, renew the heart, recover the mind, and restore the soul.

When I rendered the being of God a fairytale, I was projecting the way my husband was treating me and the mess of his brokenness (as well as my own) onto God. In fact I had abandoned God and replaced him with a human idol. It was my story I was banking on, myself and my husband I was counting on.

"Don't you think God is just a fairy tale?" I threw out the figurine of Jesus. I had thrown God out of the throne room of my heart. I considered the moment when my husband and I were in intensive care after his first accident. The priest from our church came to the room to pray with us and encourage us. We shared some Bible passages that were giving us great comfort.

As I reflected on this life episode now in 2012, I prayed, "Show me, God, what I believed then and what I believed in! What did I believe about you? How did I know you?"

I saw how I trusted in my incomplete and broken self and my incomplete and broken husband. Years before, in high school and from then on to increasing depths, I had abandoned God and forfeited myself. I was the one who tried to contain God in a fairy-tale role in my life, in my story. It was vital for me to come heart to heart with the real God; it was imperative that I comprehend that I needed him.

I had cast God in the role of fairy Godfather. My husband-prince that I held up as my king abandoned me. When I, the disrespected and rejected queen, was kept in a lonely tower; I blamed my fairy Godfather. God allowed this fairy tale to play out, and all fairy tales have a dark side.

God was not, is not a fairy-tale God. He could not and cannot be relegated to a fantasy world or restricted to some role I assign him. And that is not what I needed. I needed and need an almighty God, a loving and capable God. God allowed my choices and the choices of others to bring me to a place where adversity was harsh and I ran out of myself. A shell of red granite grew around my betrayed and wounded, broken and sinful heart. I refused to pray to this God who didn't seem to care.

In order for me to know this unconditionally loving, true and redeeming God, a God that is real and will not be—indeed, cannot be—restricted and cast in a minor role, it was necessary for me to become acquainted with adversity and my authentic self. God was/is the lead character. There is no other. It was/is his story and I am his daughter, his princess who wears biking shoes, trail-running shoes, and hiking boots; has varicose veins, grey, coarse hair, and wrinkles; bites her nails, trips on rocks and tree roots, and her own feet. You see, he is my Father in heaven, my Father in heaven who is real and draws near. I am his child. He loves me and I adore him. He has no competition. He was the baby in the manger, the young twelve-year-old in the temple, the carpenter at the workbench, the teacher on the hillside, the friend of the twelve, the man on the donkey, the Lord breaking bread, the One, fully God and fully man, who wore a crown of thorns, was nailed to a tree, this Jesus who died and was buried and was raised from the dead.

Angels did sing. Shepherds did kneel. Wise men did bring gifts. The Christmas story is real, but it does not end in the manger bed. It continues on the cross on a hill, a grave in a garden, and at the right hand of God seated on the throne. I threw God out of my fairy tale. He kept me in his story to show up in my life and make himself known to me as my real God and heavenly Father. God can penetrate granite. He wants to be known. And when you know him, everything changes.

Nothing in this sinful world that we messed-up humans live in can satisfy our deepest needs or rescue us from destruction. God is the real deal. And you can connect with him just as you are. There is no need to impress God; he already loves you like crazy. No matter what kind of hand you are dealt, whether you outright cheat or do as best you can to do the right thing, you can't win the game. The real King of Hearts trumps all.

I remembered how Beth had untangled the message in the dramatic moment when I had thrown out the baby Jesus: "You discarded a concept unsuitable for Christian maturity. It was a naïve concept. It was a rejection of a naiveté and innocence. You discounted naiveté. You discarded religion." I threw out a clay figurine and a limiting simplistic awareness of who God was. To live life, I needed more. A naïve concept of faith would not suffice on the worldwide stage of adversity. "You were designed to be in ministry. To be in ministry, you needed to know deeper adversity." I needed to know raw suffering and realize my own weaknesses and brokenness. In no other way could I identify with the suffering of Christ and the suffering of fellow human beings. "You rejected something that would not work for you."

BREAKING THE HEART OF GOD

When we lived in our second home, I had thrown out *Die Heilige Schrift*— "the holy writings"—my Bible written in German. I no longer believed Psalm 139, the Psalm I had discovered in the Bible and had read over and over again. The pages were even worn. The Bible stories I had learned and rehearsed year in and year out as I grew up were stories on the outside. I threw out my concept of what this all meant. I opened a door to allow a dark shadow to come in. Evil thought it had been summoned, yet my scream informed Evil otherwise. Now, on this night, decades after the shadow had fled and as I wrote out the account of things, I realized someone must have been praying.

I had cut and shortened my wedding dress so I would have a dress to wear for an Easter Sunday. Beth helped me to unravel the meaning of my actions. My marriage was a sham, a mockery, a fraud. Symbolically, I would wear my disgrace. I would display my disgrace, my humiliation. I felt so violated; I almost heaped violation and shame on myself. I destroyed a valued object. "You want to make a joke of me; I'll make a joke of myself."

There was that story on the front page of the newspaper so many years ago and the ensuing desperate thoughts of suicide. My whole meaning had been derived from Bob and when he did not speak of me in the article at all, he did not acknowledge my sacrifice. He denied my sacrifice. It meant nothing to him; I meant nothing to him. Even now, it is not revenge I seek. I do not want hurt or harm to come to anyone. It is not that I refuse to forgive. I had mistakenly held onto the belief that my unconditional love, my personal sacrifice, had been for nothing. I had thought that if only Bob would say he was sorry, it would give meaning to it all.

I had thrown out my high school yearbooks, which had been important to me, as all my friends had been. I threw out those yearbooks with all of the paragraphs of kind messages recorded on every page, just as I had thrown out the photo album my parents had assembled for me and the one of photos I had taken. At some point, and I am not sure when, I threw out my wedding pictures. What worth did any of these things have? What difference did any of it make? There was no meaning, no worth to any of it. My whole meaning had been derived from my husband and when he took that, I had no meaning left; no hope remained. It wasn't anger, but a desperate hopelessness, a sense of meaninglessness. I had given my all for my husband and he had forsaken me. This was a very dark time in my life. Those who knew me and spent time with me did not know. I kept it hidden. I kept it secret. I protected my husband and I protected my children.

I had written in my journal after a particular session with Beth that had brought out so many of these jpegs of my past and the realization of their meaning. I wrote, "I feel that after this session, this is indeed the week I need to visit the places where I lived in order to go deep and to let go." To go and see and ask: What are my stories? What are my moments? What was it like to be me in this place? To pray for clarity, pray to see what God sees, and to confess all that I must confess.

I betrayed God. I am a sinner. I know this full well. I also know full well the pain I felt, the anguish I knew when my husband would not return to me. The point I want to make here is that my pain in my marriage helps me, to some small degree, to comprehend how we break the heart of God. How painful it is for us to be rejected, to be betrayed. How distressing to love again and again and more and more and to give more and more, wanting to be valued, appreciated, aching for our mate to return to us. Yes, I have broken the heart of God. Oh, how I have not embraced his sacrifice. I know my husband could never find any woman who loved him more than I or any woman who would sacrifice as much as I. Yes, my heart was broken, and I have broken the heart of God. I have not embraced his sacrifice. Time and time again, I have abandoned him and forsaken him, and I have been ungrateful for all he is and all he has done for me. I stood accused, guilty and deserving of everything awful. I gave up on myself. I gave up on God. Yet God did not turn from me. He did not give up on me.

I recalled an evening when I was alone in my apartment. The girls were in college by that time. I was concerned for Joy, whose heart was breaking at the end of a relationship. Before I knew it, I found myself on the floor crying. I would do anything. I would do absolutely anything that would protect my daughter, all my children, from such pain as I had known. I would do whatever it would take to save them from such anguish. In this, I understood to a small degree; I had a small glimpse. I became somewhat aware of how God would do and did whatever it would take to keep us near to him. He knew that the worst thing that could happen to us was to be apart from him. To be separated from him would be the worst thing, the most awful thing that could ever happen to us. And he did exactly what it would take. He gave his life so we would not have to be separated from him.

THE POTTER, THE CLAY, AND THE REMAKE

When I abandoned my understanding of God, when I rejected any and all concepts I had of him, he remained the *Psalm 139 God.* And in his great and generous wisdom and grace, he used my mess to mold me and shape me and make me stronger.

Not until I ran out of myself, realized my own brokenness, and comprehended my need for God, could I—would I—let him into my heart, the center of my spirit, my very being, where my emotions, thoughts, motivations, courage, and action come to life.

———————

It was as if the hand of Jesus were on the doorknob on the door to my life center. He had long ago turned the knob so that the latch was released and the door would open instantly at a light touch of invitation.

———————

The clay pot rejected the Potter, but the Potter just kept working on the clay until she became more and more pliable in his capable and loving hands. God took the obscene mess I had made of the clay pot and shaped a beautiful, one-of a-kind Remake of Mary. (Isaiah 64:8 NIV)

MESSAGE ALERT IN THE MIDDLE OF THE NIGHT

After working on this book late into the night, I had trouble falling asleep. I finally drifted off only to wake up again at 1:00 a.m. or so and again at about 3:00. *Forgive them, for they do not know what they are doing!* popped up in my mind like an alert box on the computer screen.

"*Now,* what button did I hit? Where did *that* message come from? And just how do I get rid of it?" I tried to click it off the screen. The box flashed off and then immediately popped back into view. *Forgive them, for they do not know what they are doing!*

"Jesus, just how did *you* manage to say that? Surely those who falsely accused you knew what they were doing. Surely anyone who used such a hideous means of murder knew to some degree, had *some* notion, that it was wrong. Surely their arrogance, sick politics and heart-numbing greed were staring them in the face. (And I count myself among them.)"

Forgive them, for they do not know what they are doing! The unsettling pop-up message continued and was getting irritating. *Did you know, Mary?* (Pause.) *Mary, did you know?*

I thought about my behavior, my living, my sinning, my avoidance, my denial, my excessive passivity, my reluctance to insert myself, and unaware-ness of my frailties—with great potential for harm—that I had hidden in the crevasse. Yes, I knew; but I didn't know. I needed help. Forty years later I finally began to understand the feelings, the personality, the frailty, the weaknesses, the okay human emotions, the confusion, the prevailing denial. Something had a kind of grip on me. What was it? I didn't want to be in this place.

Jesus said, "Father, forgive them, for they do not know what they are doing." (Luke 23:34 NIV)

For so long—since lessons in Sunday school—I accepted this state-ment made by Jesus. I knew he had said it. The people pounding the nails into his hands, the world standing by doing nothing. Did we not know he was the very son of God? Did we not know that our thoughts and our actions were criminal? You, me, we all had blinders on. I remembered my life before I had met this Jesus.

Evil is present. Evil is what God hates. Evil is what works in us, tricks us, blinds us, deceives us, and confuses us. Evil is a harmful, conniving, disgusting, deplorable menace that causes great damage. It is the snare that binds and blinds and holds people in bondage.

Surely someone who is narcissistic knows to some degree that he or she is dealing out pain and disregard. Surely I saw my frailty and knew my faults and comprehended my wrongdoing. There must have been some glimmer of awareness.

You know, it is only God working in us that can remove the blinders. It is all about God revealing this truth and God making it evident, often working through others to clean our lenses so we can see inside ourselves. This is one of the illuminating messages I knew I needed. The piece of this weaving, the levels, the layers, the back and forth, the knotted back side, the adulteress, the adulterer, the scum of the earth.

I learned more about narcissism. The Wikipedia website pulls together a tight knit weave of concepts about narcissism and codependency. This verbal snapshot is interesting to consider: *In everyday speech, "narcissism" often means egoism, vanity, conceit, or simple selfishness. Applied to a social group, it is sometimes used to denote elitism or an indifference to the plight of others. In psychology, the term is used to describe both normal self-love and unhealthy self-absorption due to a disturbance in the sense of self....Codependency may also be characterized by denial, low self-esteem, excessive compliance, or control patterns. Narcissists are considered to be natural magnets for the codependent.* As mentioned earlier, this online Free Encyclopedia also states that attributes of a narcissist can be difficulty with empathy, and denial of remorse or gratitude.

I wondered if my excessive passivity was fertile soil for an acquired co-dependency in the dynamics of my marital relationship. A person could conclude that my ex and I allowed the worst in each other. It did look like two broken people in a broken relationship with each other.

Forgive them, for they do not know not what they are doing!

I needed a God of grace and love and compassion, a God who would forgive me. I needed God in my life. I needed the wise counsel of a psychologist and the encouragement of friends and family. I am still broken, but the pieces are coming together. I needed help to go deeper, to see myself, to go into the crevasse with an informed light to help me to look at the formations, the crevices, the ledges, and the ice without condemnation and shame. My ex-husband was and is broken. *Forgive them, for they do not know not what they are doing!*

Jesus gasps. He struggles in pain to take a breath. He whispers from the cross; the Holy Spirit whispers. God is stretching out his arms and saying, "Come to me. I forgive you. Come to me; I forgive you. Come to me. I forgive you, even though you don't see all you have done. And now go—and forgive them, for they, too, do not know what they have done or what they do."

Forgive them, for they do not know what they are doing: does it mean we are guiltless? Does it mean we are off the hook? Does it mean we are not accountable? Does it mean we are home free? Does it mean we do not have to apologize to those we have injured? No! We are required to say we are sorry to God and to those we have hurt and offended. As broken and sinful people, we are in desperate need of that divinely enabled repentance. (And, we would all benefit greatly from professionally guided self-discovery.)

PARABLE OF THE PYTHON (OR, "THERE'S A SNAKE IN MY HOUSE!")

I hated worms and I didn't care for snakes. (Snakes were far worse.) My dislike for worms and snakes was pretty extreme. I didn't want to see worms, touch them, or be anywhere near them. When my daughter was in grade school, she took a rubber fishing lure worm (one without the hooks) and laid it carefully over a tack on the large bulletin board in our kitchen. Then she took another rubber worm and tossed it in the fresh, foamy, very sudsy dishwater in the sink. I entered the kitchen to start doing the dishes and put my hands in the water. *Yuck! Oh man! Gross! Katyyyyyy!*

Katy said, "Mom, you have to get used to them."

During one of my childhood family vacations, we traveled out east. One stop was Cape Cod, where we used hand lines to fish for flounder. Hand over hand, we would pull the fish into the boat. The recommended bait was sea worms, about a foot or so long; they were reddish brown, as I remember, with light-colored, wriggly legs all along their sides. Dad would cut them into three-inch pieces and would bait our hooks. Yuck. I could look at them, but kept my feet on the seat of the boat so the worms absolutely would not touch me as they squirmed on the wooden floor. I still can't believe I even remained in the boat. We did indeed catch a lot of flounder. Mom fried the floured flounder fillets in yummy butter for breakfast. Oh, my.

On a particularly rainy day when I lived in my apartment and two of my kids were off to college, there was a worm that somehow got in my front door. Just who let that critter in? I didn't even hear the knock. Anyway, I jumped back when I noticed it as I headed out the door for work. He was on the carpet. Good grief. I found a yardstick or something and carefully picked him up and put him outside. It was dramatic. I told my friend and secretary about it and the next day, she gave me a red plastic watering can in the shape of a giant worm. She said it was in honor of the killer worm I had rescued. I laughed so hard.

Then, there was a time when I was taking my first granddaughter for a walk. She was maybe three years old. We saw a snake trying again and again to wind up a flat, inclined cement curb on a neighborhood street. He would try to climb up and would slide back down sideways. I thought to myself, "Oh, man! I can't believe I am going to rescue this snake! Yuck. Okay." I noticed a small pile of dry grass clippings close by. I picked up a handful and sprinkled them in the snake's desired path. As soon as I placed the clippings on the curb, he slithered up it and slipped toward the nearby garden in the neighbor's front lawn. (I didn't even like the word "slithered.")

One October, one of my favorite months to bike off-road, I saw what I thought was a long, very straight, black stick across the limestone trail. As I got closer, I realized it was a snake sunning itself on the trail. I turned on the path and went back the other way.

My brother told me that once when he was biking, a crow dropped a snake, two-and-a-half to three feet long. It landed on his back, around his neck. I hated snakes.

Well, that was then and now is now. At age fifty-nine I got a ball python. His name is Marty—a male version of the combination of Mary and Martha. (My Labrador is Boaz and my cat is Gideon, so I wanted a biblical name for my snake.) I can hardly believe it. All those who know me can hardly believe it. There is a snake in my house!

As I was on this journey back to my lonely and painful past, for some reason I was sensing a lessening of my phobia for snakes. When I went to my twelve-year-old granddaughter's grandparent's day at her school, her teacher took their classroom pet, a corn snake, out of its glass cage. Actually, he was quite pretty. (Did I just call a snake pretty?) "Come on, Mimi," my granddaughter said. She took my hand and pulled me gently from my seat next to hers and then led me to the front of the group gathered around the snake winding itself around the teacher's fingers. I instructed my granddaughter, "You stay close to me!" As I was actually about to reach out courageously and touch the snake, the teacher said, "Well, time to put Helix back in his house." I really was ready to give it a try.

A month or so later, my other granddaughter was having a reptile-themed birthday party and I sensed I should be there. I wanted to help my daughter with the dozen or so kids, and I thought this might be a moment in conquering this phobia. The owner of the reptile specialty shop brought about a dozen reptiles to the house and very gently and calmly provided a safe, non-risky environment for the girls and boys to touch or hold the snakes, lizards, geckos, and bearded dragons. I held some different snakes and even had a ball python around my neck while I told this lover and keeper of reptiles to stay close by.

About three to four weeks after the reptile adventure, I ordered a snake. He arrived on December 20, 2011. Marty is a beautiful, four-month-old cinnamon ball python. His markings are amazing; his face is cute. The cat would like him to come out and play. The lab seems not to be sure what the heck is in the large glass box, but when I bring home a rat or two for Marty's once-a-week lunch, Bo is pretty intrigued with the smells and sounds coming from the paper bag. I try to cradle Marty once a week, but not on feeding day. Snakes are not slimy; they are smooth and soft and very neat to touch. It is quite amazing to hold one.

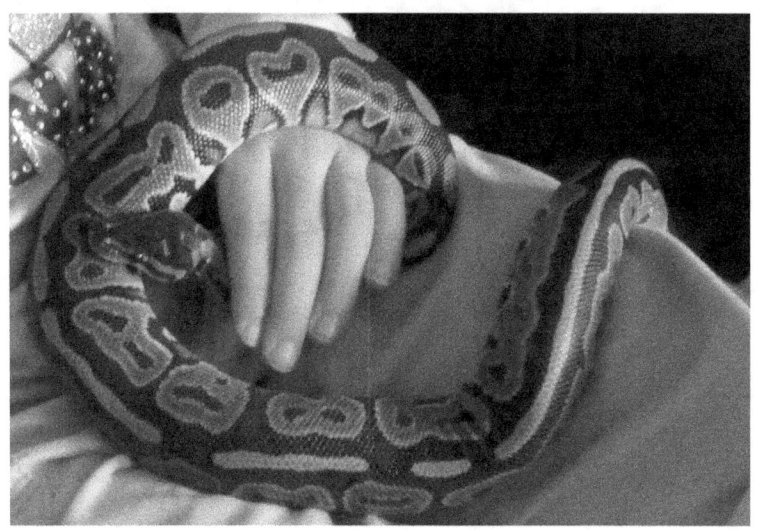

Marty Held Gently By My Granddaughter 2012

Once fearful of sharing my full, authentic self and of telling my story to anyone for forty years, I am newly free. I needed best friends to encourage me to tell my story. I needed someone compassionate and knowledgeable to listen to my stories and guide my recovery. I needed this person to be close by and let me know it was okay. I needed her to tell me I don't have to protect my ex-husband any more. I needed good friends to listen and care and still love me. Family and friends listened to my story and did not abandon me, but loved me all the more and often shared their stories, too. I can share all of my personality parts with those near to me, and it is good. The lonely and painful memories are losing their sting and I am learning not to shove selected emotions into a cage. I am not afraid of being known and the experience of telling my story is quite amazing and smoother than I ever imagined.

No, I am not going to let Marty loose in my house. At least, I do not plan to, no matter how much Gideon meows and pleads with me.

13
COSTLY EMPOWERMENT, EMANCIPATION, AND LIFE LEARNING

EMPOWERMENT TO RELEASE THE OFFENDER

When I dated Ted, the third dating referral, I had put him first and had disregarded self and boundaries because of the age-old desire to please and make and keep someone happy. Against my better judgment and the advice I received in a still, small voice, I lent him money. I knew it was a very dumb move on my part. Extremely dumb. I did eventually catch on and drew a line, stood my ground, and ended the relationship. Beth commented, "You are easily exploited." I told Beth that it was a concern for me in future dating and possible marriage. She responded, "It is a weak spot in your fortress."

And here is a frustrating, hair-pulling, ah!-screaming, head-on-the-wall-pounding, infuriating factor: When I later told this Mr. Narcissistic that I truly needed the money he owed me for this and this and this, he responded, "Mary, who is your source? God is my source."

I told him, "You broke this promise and that promise."

"Mary, for the life of me, I can't remember. Besides, I told you we would disappoint one another." This warning of future disappointment reminded me of my ex-husband's tactic of warning me about future infidelity as if to say, *I am telling you up front, so that makes it acceptable.* In this case, it was Ted Narcissistic's *get out of jail free card.*

"You are responsible to pay me the money you promised to return," I told Ted.

"Mary, I am accountable to God. I have moved on; you should, too."

I was communicating with him via email, so no; I did not punch him in the face. I have to start making homemade bread again. Punching dough is great therapy! Better yet, I'll go lift weights at the YMCA.

Then it hit me! This guy was telling me that he is accountable to God and does not need to pay me back. This was like my ex saying he was accountable to God and did not have to say to me that he was sorry, because God had forgiven him.

They were both behaving in an exploitive manner and dismissed their responsibilities. In essence, they were speaking prophetically to me. Yes, they are and will be accountable to God. (Likewise will I.) That is like daring lightning to strike you while you are on a golf course, under an isolated tree, standing in a puddle of water, and holding your wedge in the water.

Beth shared this: "So, in response to being exploited, it is natural to empower yourself. After victimization, people desire to accomplish something that is empowering. What is more empowering than to let go?" There was nothing wrong with the athletic and collegiate means I typically grabbed onto. And yet, the truest empowerment is to let it go. I am not saying that you "get over it." You and I have to work through it, but then we are empowered to let it go.

True empowerment is the God-given ability to let go of all trespasses against you. Some people may retreat. Some may retreat to self-medication. Beth added that the average person who has experienced what I experienced would have retreated. "You are not average; you strive and accomplish things. Yet everyone has the ability to let go." And I remember the earlier learning that love spilled out is never wasted. All love and wisdom is from God. He will harvest the field watered with spilled-out love. That which can truly empower us is to let go. And when there is a reminder of the offense, to be determined to forgive and let go again.

Green and Lawrenz explained it this way: *The living of forgiveness challenges the forgiver to continue to release the offender each time there is a reminder of wrongdoing and to resolve the various emotional reactions that occur with each reminder.* (p. 60)

I wrote this book to encourage others to work through and release. I wanted to show others the empowerment of letting go and finding freedom in that. It is part of the forgiveness process.

I am finally in the place of knowing that those who have caused great injury cannot or will not see what they have done. They will not say they are sorry. Their answer remains the same: no. It is possible, maybe even likely, that they are not sorry. I lay my sin, my shame, my devoted love at the cross. My sins are forgiven. My shame is lifted and is no more. My love spent is mingled with the love of Christ, and God will use it. Spilled-out love is never wasted. It is never a wasted expense. When I (and when you) recognize this truth, bitterness is dissolved. God can move us into a place of empowerment *to let go*.

Love spilled out is never wasted. It is never a wasted expense.

MOUNTAIN STREAMS

Hours before sunrise, my daughter and I began our climb of Longs Peak in Colorado. After a short time, we heard the peaceful sound of rushing water. In the darkness with only our headlamps, we couldn't see the water beyond the trees to the left of us; but it was lovely and delightful to hear.

On our trek back down the mountain, we stopped to rest by a very small mountain stream. We filtered clear and icy water from the stream into our water bottles. It revived and energized us to continue down the mountain.

And here I was on the downward climb with a headlamp shedding light on my journey. A stream of memories rushed through my mind. As I filtered out the contaminants, I could take in the meaning and life learning within the river of stories. It became a refreshing drink of learning and new freedoms:

My path toward alienation from self began in high school. I disconnected from my dreams and from my own identity in pursuit of an identity with Bob and his dreams. The more that pursuit was blocked, the more disconnected I became. I slipped into a downward spiral of losing myself. In order to lose myself, I had to lose God. To keep going in this relationship, I had to lose myself, including losing the God-piece that was woven into me. I taught myself not to believe. I entertained no identity but to exist for my husband. In doing so, I shed my confidence, my goals, and my desires. The only identity was that of him: Bob, loving me. This was the very programming many women have from the fall, the "curse" of women: her affection shall be for her husband. She pursues this idyllic affection to an unhealthy extreme and to her own detriment. The loss of identity, self-worth, values, and even killing God in me was part of that desperate act. At a developmental level, I had to kill the God in me to go down this road of rejecting my identity and abandoning myself. The absolute truth is: I cannot have an identity without or apart from a concept of God. When I reject God, I am rejecting my own identity. Further down the road of despair, I gave up on God. Why does God let this happen?

I couldn't persist in the sickness of that relationship, which led me to the point of rejecting God. And God allowed me to go there to see this darkness. A merciful God says, "I will let you be turned over to this pursuit and your abandonment of me so that you might come back." The perfect, white-picket-fence picture was not working for me as I had imagined it. God was part of this perfect picture in my mind, but the picture was not working. I tried to push God out of the picture. In such a place, I didn't belong to myself anymore; I belonged to this pursuit. I idolized the idea that my idol would love me.

All else goes numb, and the pursuit becomes a substitute for God. It seems we have a programmed awareness of intimate unity. We are meant—wired—to be in relationship and in a relationship with God. This is not a defect; it is not a faulty dependency. It is as if we are Eve, wired to seek out affection, intimacy, closeness, and unity with her husband. The "after the fall effect" reveals itself when the wiring of this programming is short circuited and we keep pursuing this affection, even when all evidence suggests there is no point. We keep up the pursuit to a point of forfeiting self and renouncing God, a sequence leading to impending electrocution of self. Women are oriented to pursue even when it is clearly self-destructive to deny reality, ourselves, others, and God. Eve pursued even though it led to destruction. Adam let her do so to the detriment of self and others. God's plan is not thwarted. He had a plan for redemption before the first day of creation. And in his plan he forgives me, forgives us and empowers us to forgive. The contaminants are filtered out; the water purified. Our relationship with God is restored.

Powerful teachings from Beth became clearer still. The prayers she offered and the wisdom, love, and faith she shared, were abundant in a very remarkable way. They would stretch my comprehension of my present and my past. When I read through my records of our conversations, new learning would break in.

DO I GET BACK ON THIS HORSE?

As I relaxed in the waiting area before a session with Beth, I recalled a story she had shared. Her once-trusted horse had bucked her all the way around the riding arena. It was a frightening experience, and she was injured. Her horse did not keep her safe. This was the tough question she faced, as any other rider would after such an encounter: Do I get back on this horse?

Sometime later, she was watching her trainer and others during a state horse-riding competition. She saw three "dumps" and fifteen or so incidents where a horse was not keeping its rider safe. Others had painful and frightening experiences like hers. It was true for me as well. I have learned that many other women have been hurt in situations like mine.

Throughout the chronic infidelity of my husband, I kept getting back on the horse. After years of emotional burial and relationship risk denial, I finally faced the obvious message from his track record that my husband did not keep me safe. He did not care that I could fall or suffer internal injuries. He did not protect me. How could I trust that there would not be a repeat of last time—and the time before that, and the time before that? When he would once again not quit his affair, he made it clear that my welfare and my love were not something he considered worth keeping safe. When would I learn that it was not safe to get back on this horse?

READ THE RED LETTER

It is important to read the Red Letter. A Red Letter is costly, so make the learning count!

In one of my meetings with Beth, I talked about the time- line of things, including my passage through becoming physically fit: swimming, biking, running, the Tinman Triathlon, my affair, the separation and divorce. Once again my affair came up in our conversation. Beth spoke of the need for us to revisit that and process that time in my life. It would be right and beneficial not to view the situation through a lens of shame. To render judgment and descend into shame before sitting with the situation and seeing the why of it all would choke off the potential learning and opportunity to heal and to grow and to see once again how God takes our messes and works them out for good. It would be important to allow myself to see the situation from all angles, and even see the good that came from it. I learned that it was critical to examine the teaching that

God allowed to happen in the affair. He lets his wisdom come through to us even in things like this.

I wrote this book about infidelity to help others come out of the darkness and be known and to know they matter to God. God knew that Gary was in my path. We have a tendency to villainize adulterers. Beth commented that the affair helped me to believe in myself again and to see that I was attractive to someone. It was meeting a human need. I had lost my identity and essentially had withdrawn from relationships with others. The affair initiated my search for identity and allowed me to separate myself from my marriage situation. I found out that I could be someone other than a person who just existed for Bob, who had betrayed me from the very beginning. To him, the marriage was a farce even before we said, "I do." I could have desires apart from him—the desire to be loved, to be physically fit and attractive, to be wanted. This was part of my struggle out. I was not a polygamist. For me to have an affair, I had already finally given up on the marriage. Bob's persistence in pushing me to have an affair only underscored his failure to care for me. For me, this wasn't for sex or payback or a "what the hell, he is screwing around all the time." I was starving for a relationship and my marriage was meaningless. When he said, "I do," he meant, "I won't."

I recalled when I was on the last leg of my triathlon and my husband was once again downplaying my worth and drawing attention to himself. I thought, *This is for me. I needed this.* The triathlon and the perseverance and individual accomplishment to get it done were *positive* steps in the struggle out of my suffocating relationship.

Beth commented that I needed to be spiritually and emotionally separate, to break that bond that was choking me. I needed to break out, to climb out. I was desperate to get out in order to survive. My affair became part of that survival.

It was complicated. It was misguided and morally shameful. It dishonored God. Adultery is a great and awful sin. I have confessed my sin to others, to the ones I have injured, and to God. I promptly said I was sorry many years ago, and I say it again. I still struggle not to burn myself at the stake for it, but Jesus would say: let him who has no sin light the first match. He doesn't want me to set myself on fire, either.

Beth reminded me about the account of Mary Magdalene, who faced a riotous stoning, and about the woman at the well, who Jesus spoke with. He did not condemn them. He knew them. He knew their stories. He knows our weaknesses and he knows what we are made of. He knows our stories, and he offers his love and forgiveness.

In this corridor of my memory, I observed a sad reality: I withdrew love from myself. All those years I did not love me. I never withdrew my love from my husband, even though again and again and again and again he was unfaithful to me. He did not treat me like his wife. *When God instructs us to consider others better than ourselves, he is not telling us to consider ourselves of little worth. God created me in his image, and he paid a great price for my salvation: he assigned me permanent worth.* Nothing I can do or say can add or subtract from his great love for me or the value he assigns me. It is my purpose to remain mindful and to take to heart that nothing anyone else can do or say can subtract from my self-worth. I gave my husband far too much power and credibility. I did not extend kindness or love to myself.

Yes, the affair I had was a sin and a toxic drink. Nothing makes it right, and there were ugly and painful consequences. And I have beaten myself up for a long time. The experience was far too costly not to consider the learning to be derived from it.

14
AN INCUBATION PERIOD CHOSEN BY GOD AND HEALING WISDOM OFFERED THROUGH A FRIEND

Learning from Beth, July 18, 2011: It was an anointing of the Holy Spirit for you to share your story at this time in your life. You were at a point of clarity, maturity and strength now. Sharing your story years ago before now would be given over to pursuit, a compromise in identity. One more voice other than God would have confused you. God brought someone now through your daughter. He saw it as your protection and incubation. God was okay for you being alone in it. God brought himself to you. He chose to let you walk it alone.

If you lose yourself, you need to find yourself. You need to own that you completely lost yourself. A man in your life, this second Bob, others you have dated, triggered a weakness to lose self again. You were still finding yourself before. You forfeited yourself when you got married. <u>*God doesn't want you to forfeit yourself again.*</u> *There is much more for you to do. God wired you, prepared you for your calling. He worked on and developed your steadfastness and independence. God honed your tenacity, great mind, compassion and your servant's heart. Now there is nothing in your way. There is much still for you to do. I know your self-doubt is gone. In any relationship the guy will have to get on board with your agenda. You don't have to be flexible and make yourself fit theirs. Take confidence to a new level. A man opposite of Bob. A best friend for your support system. Supportive of your mission and your calling. It is not about trying to follow him. Love me and like me.*

As you date and meet others go in as you are and the right man will be attracted to you just the way you are. "Insert yourself!" has become a spiritual and social mantra for you.

When you meet men, stand firm in what you are! Don't waste time with someone you have to convince or pursue!

We can have expectation in relationships, a kind of misguided expectation. Expecting Bob to care for you was like someone in a wheelchair and you wanted him to get up and walk. Add to that feeling less of a person if someone doesn't love you. "If they loved me they would get up and walk. I know he could get up and walk if he wanted. I am going to do everything I need to do; then he will get up and walk." You can work harder and harder and it still won't happen.

Bob was an oppressor who caused great injury and has no awareness of the depth of pain and despair he caused. This and all you went through hold great sorrow. He is incapable of figuring out where you are, what you went through and how to have empathy. I (Beth) believe he knows full well that what he did was wrong and it is unbearable to him. See him as incapable and <u>find release from trying to get a different answer.</u>

There is a female type of arrogance, "You will love me!" There is a needing to be loved. You need to accept that they don't love you and be okay with that. Insisting he love you, you made Bob a false idol and pursued him to a point of laying down yourself. You conformed yourself to what you thought he wanted.

When I first journaled the above, I realized that I would need to insert myself as I moved on in the mission to write and publish this book. Not everyone will love me, not all will agree with me; and some people who love me will not agree with me. And I will need to stand firm, strong, and confident.

I told Beth about my unexpected response to seeing Bob at my granddaughter's swimming meet. I first saw my kids. As I approached that area of the pool deck, I saw Bob and Joan, their daughter, and her fiancé. I was not sure how I felt. Bob was smiling. I think he just happened to be turning around and was smiling at the time in response to the conversation he was engaged in when I approached. He usually does not acknowledge my presence or respond. He moves someplace else, distances himself. Again, he just moved away.

Beth coached, "Start where you are. Not running, welcome the feelings. Bring negative feelings in and *eat them.* Let them teach you. Allow them without anxiety. Stay contemplative."

I saw the humiliated young Mary in the hallway again at the apartment. I saw the young me in the room at the ambulance station. Bob and the other guys were there; Rita was there. I walked out. Then I was once again in the parking lot when I was leaving one of Joy's swimming meets. Katy gave me a hug good-bye and then as I went to my car, alone, she ran after Joan and hugged her. Joan put her arm around my little girl and they laughed together.

Then I thought again about the recent swimming meet. I tasted the feeling of rejection from Bob as I saw him. I felt my shoulders slump. I felt shorter, smaller; and I felt like I was on the outside.

Beth then said, "Breathe in this murky water. Where do you feel it?"

"I feel it in my chest, heaviness. Why can't I release it? What is this about rejection for me? I think I always felt excluded, like I was on the outside."

Beth commented, "It is the old you. 'I will do everything I can to earn it, Bob's love, respect and affection.'"

She asked, "How do you respond to someone who treats you as if you mean nothing? This is a weak spot in your fortress."

I see it and know it now, for God has made a way for me to climb down into the crevasse and uncover, discover, and recover. In order to recover I was required to take the light down into the deep places, dark places, the hidden parts of me. I need to know about my weak places. I realized, too, that as I learned more about the real me, I gained a more profound knowing of God.

There is a place where we hide parts of our authentic selves, our fears, flaws, frailties, and failings. We do this sometimes to protect ourselves and others. There is shame, sadness, despair, anger…emotions we have no name for, emotions we never learned how to express. These emotions, buried and left to linger, cause decay just below the surface. Things can get ugly. In my situation, seeing Bob and his wife stirred up those old emotions. I could almost taste them. I have eaten them and I can recognize the taste now. I will be present and see myself on the inside. I will choose a different response. (Sometimes I guess the old response might be almost automatic. Then, I will choose to change my response.)

How will I choose to respond to someone who treats me as if I mean nothing?

Following the incubation period chosen by the Creator, I was enabled to find release. My ex-husband is incapable of saying he is sorry. I will no longer try to get a different answer. He is not capable of affirming the depth of my love or my sacrifice. I do not need him to say he is sorry and I do not need him to acknowledge my expense of unconditional love. I have found release. Through Beth the Holy Spirit gave me wisdom to guide me through this process. To paraphrase Isaiah 50:4, *the Sovereign Lord gave her an instructed tongue to know the word that sustains the weary. He wakens her morning by morning, wakens her ear to listen like one being taught.*

15
STONES AND STORIES ONCE
LOST ARE FOUND

IF YOU STOP PLOWING AND PICK UP
THE STONES
WHAT WILL YOU FIND?

It was the early 1920s. Grandpa Sam was a young man plowing the fields along the Rock River. Every so often, he would stop the tractor and step down. He walked a few steps and bent down over the freshly tilled earth. He picked up a small stone and then let it drop back to the ground. Another stone lay close by. He picked up the second stone and removed damp dirt as he rubbed the stone between his thumb and fingers. This one looked and felt different. It was smooth, with a defined shape; it was the size of a silver dollar, but not round. He stepped back to the plow and continued working. After a time, he saw another stone about the size of a half dollar, stepped down, bent over the ground, and picked it up. This one was smooth just like the second one, but it was rounded on the top like a mushroom. Another was shaped like an evergreen tree—more like an arrow, actually. One stone was a deep gray, the other more the color of a duck egg. The young farmer put the arrowheads in his deep shirt pocket and got back to the plow.

As the day wore on, he stopped and drank from the water jar tucked next to him on the seat of the tractor. He once again looked down at the earth, now prepared for planting. He noticed a much larger stone of a deep, salt-and-pepper gray, as long as the diameter of a softball. One end had a chisel-like edge; the opposite side had a very smooth carved groove. I can comfortably cup the grooved side in my hand. (I was holding it during the time I was at the computer keyboard.) The stone was probably a Late or Middle Archaic axe, some 5,000 years old. It was granite. My sister also has such a stone that is twice as large and twice as heavy.

My dad knows a lot about a lot, so I asked him once again, "So Dad, what were these stones used for anyway?" The arrowheads that Sam found on the farm were probably used to kill birds and small game, others for larger game. Still other stone tools were shaped to scrape and clean the hides of game. Some of the archaic stones were designed for harvesting, scrapping, or carving; while others were shaped for cutting, drilling, and even writing. Others, a rare find, were carved as multi-purpose tools with a scribe point for writing, a serrated edge for sawing or cutting, and a side with shavers to shape arrows, perhaps. Similar stone tools have been found for people groups from a number of time periods.

I have fifty-one arrowheads arranged on a smooth, finished piece of wood. (It is actually the front of an old dresser drawer.) The arrowheads are attached with chlorinated paraffin and have been mounted this way for about forty or forty-five years. Mom and Dad gave them to me to hang in my home. I wrote this as I was looking at them hanging on the wall in my computer room. Including the displays my parents, my brother, and my sister have, there are about two hundred twenty arrowheads and stone tools. Dad said Grandpa told him one out of every four times he climbed down from the tractor to check out a particular stone he had uncovered, he would find an arrowhead. So to collect these archaic artifacts, he had to get off the tractor about eight hundred times. It took precious time and patience to discover these underground treasures that had a story to tell.

Arrowheads from the Farm

Just think of the stories of the Indian women, men, and children living along the Rock River. My grandfather grew up there and then married Grandma. You should have tasted her German potato pancakes with homemade applesauce and yummy syrup. She would use about ten pounds of potatoes and a dozen egg yolks. Then she made schaum torte from all the egg whites. My mother grew up in the farmhouse on the farm along the Rock River. My dad met my mother and fell in love with her, and he loves her still.

(I remember the night before Mother's Day, 2012. I opened the door to my parents' flat just to say hi. Mom and Dad were holding each other as they gently and tenderly danced together in front of *The Lawrence Welk Show* with its lovely music from the past. Dad is ninety-four; Mom is eighty-six. They have been married over sixty-six years.)

You can learn a lot from stories. Even stones have a story to tell about how people lived and worked and survived. Sometimes you just have to stop the plowing to look more closely at the recent or ancient artifacts you just uncovered and consider the story hidden there.

BURIED STONES AND BURIED STORIES HAVE GREAT MEANING

During weekly sessions last summer, my dear friend Beth and I, even deeper in the crevasse, were discovering rock-hard artifacts of another kind, each with a story to tell. Sometimes you need someone who knows a lot about a lot to shed some light on the findings so you can know and understand the message. As I reread and prayed through my journal entries from those summer days, I learned even more. I stopped the daily plowing and took time to consider what we had discovered, uncovered, and recovered.

It is important for sacrifice to have meaning. I did not hold onto my pain because of an interest in revenge or a refusal to forgive, but because of the importance of what the pain represents. It was important for me to remember how I deeply loved. If I remembered the pain and sacrifice for love, it meant it was not a waste of time or place or me. I needed to remember. Why? So I do not do it again? So I do not make the same mistakes? I needed to remember and understand to know that my sacrifice was not in vain. If I remembered the sacrifice, love had meaning. I couldn't walk away complete otherwise. I had to take some piece with me so I could remember that I had loved him. My love was at great expense. If I forgot, even though the memory triggered pain, it would somehow take away the meaning of my sacrifice. It was all part of the determination to justify the sacrifice.

For such a sacrifice, for such a love to be pointless or lost would be awful to endure. On what basis was this sacrifice made? This love spent? This self given out?

Beth picked up a stone from the field and rubbed the accumulated soil off of the surface: *It is never a loss when we love someone. It is never a waste of time to love someone. Still, it is a waste of time to try to 'get' someone to love you. It is a waste of time to try to get him to love you. You begin to idolize him. We need to release control over the outcome. Don't get caught up in the outcome. Manifest God by loving Bob. Bitterness is about wasted time and energy. Love is never a waste of time or energy. God takes care of the harvest. God knows what the harvest is. Bob can never say, 'I don't know what love is.' He met Mary.*

She continued: *Why is it important to love him now? "Love your enemies." Loving your enemies is the completion of the work, not just of forgiveness, but of God's love in you. You become fortified without a personal agenda. You become fortified in God's love. You are truly strong. Loving Bob makes you stronger and freer and wiser. You want to end up in a position of love.*

This learning was so valuable for me. Vengeance was never a desire of mine, nor did I play out a victim role or withhold forgiveness. Uncovering this long-buried piece helped me to understand and articulate why I hung onto the pain. I also understood why my need for Bob to say he was sorry was so pressing. If he said he was sorry, it would somehow give validity and value to my sacrifice of love and self. I see now that God maintains the value of my loving Bob. I could not get him to love me in the past and wanting him to say he was sorry was equally as hopeless, a pointless continuation of my attempt to have Bob assign value to my sacrifice. It doesn't matter if Bob does not grasp the depth of my sacrifice, my love, my unconditional love. God has seen it and He knows it. He will manage the harvest. I release that love to God, to God who is the source of love and the designer of my capacity to love.

An *aha moment* is when something new or out of focus is now made clear, or a piece previously not apparent is revealed. Something once confusing, you now understand. You are deeply moved. In all cases, discernment is increased. One of my *aha moments*: God's amazing unconditional love and his sacrifice so often go unnoticed, unrecognized, unaccepted, ignored, rejected, and mistaken. When individuals fail to or refuse to acknowledge God's generous and genuine love and costly grace, his infinite love and divine sacrifice are not made worthless. And the impact will be incredible; and the benefits will be eternal.

THREE PRECIOUS GEMS

Your kids are your purpose, meaning, and joy. They are next only to Jesus for you.

Bob and I had a shared custody arrangement on alternating weeks. Not having my children with me essentially six months out of every year was painful. This was one of the emotional stones of loss, grief, and resentment buried deep in the crevasse that required excavation, examination, and recovery.

You lost that time with your children because of him. He did *want a divorce and pushed you into a corner. He would not give up Joan, just as he felt entitled to all the others. You are a victim again because of him and his partnership with serial infidelity. Now, as a part of the consequences, you had to give up time with your children. This is very difficult for you, for your wonderful, joyful self is happiest in your mother role.*

At this time in your life, a restlessness entered in, a restless depression. You stored a resentment that it was his fault the kids were not with you, that there was separation. You held out as long as you did. It is a bitter root of isolation. You did not want to sit still with it. You fought it, coping. You never became thoroughly powerless and tried to stay ahead of the powerlessness, for the most part laying down many layers of resentment. Your buried emotions were saying, "I resent the hell out of you." Your maternal role was so huge that you battled your own anger. Your loss of self-esteem and depression became familiar and a way of life.

This anger and resentment were both powerful and difficult. Things were out of my control. If I could control anger, I would feel in control.

Beth prayed, we prayed. The Holy Spirit always comes in. God showed her my resentment. Beth sensed the Holy Spirit saying "I allowed this," and that I needed to understand that God had allowed this. She said, "Bob didn't take the kids away from you. God allowed it. You must understand. He allowed that, from the beginning of creation, the beginning of time."

Beth instructed, "I want you to process memories; journal your memories. See things differently, but remember first. It will be unpleasant. You have been trying to hold back the tide for a long time. These feelings are unpleasant." Depression, vulnerability, isolation, powerlessness, and situations out of my control were all buried in the crevasse under layer upon layer of the fermented sediment of resentment. My friend was concerned. "This will be difficult. You will probably feel depressed. Call me if you need to."

Lord, let me feel how you feel when your children are taken away. I was fearful of completing the petition. I did not want to feel that. I knew it must be awful.

Then I began to think of the times when I was separated from my children.

I would say that the time when Bob took his first mistress and me dancing when I was pregnant with my first child was where depression and resentment with regard to one or all of my three precious gems became part of my story. This scene began the first chapter of the father of my children not valuing me or honoring my role as mother and wife.

This part of the downward climb was not like finding a rare artifact or discovering an ancient arrowhead. Rather, it was like lifting up a heavy rock and finding the slugs stuck to the bottom and crawling in the wet dirt beneath.

I can still see my young daughter running after Joan in an elementary school parking lot, arm in arm with her and laughing. My daughter had just hugged me good-bye. I drove home alone. On another day, Joan came to pick up my children from our house, took my daughter's bike out of the garage, and put it into her car. Joan did not ask me or anything. She just took it. I hadn't seen what was happening until she had stashed the bike and headed down the driveway, ignoring me when I called out. She just drove away. I was angry. My rights had been violated once again. I had no control. I drove over to my ex-husband's condo, and no one was home.

I felt powerless. I picked up a huge planter that was sitting on the front step and smashed it on the ground.

Bob required the kids to call him every day, including every day when they were with me on vacation. This ticked off my lawyer. She said it was one more way for him to keep control, always control. It was particularly challenging when we were on vacation, because there were no cell phones back then. Usually I would have to search for a public phone when we were traveling. Often it meant calling at night from a phone booth by a park ranger station. The light at the phone booth attracted every mosquito in northern Wisconsin, but I always made sure the kids could call their dad.

John was three when his father and I were divorced. When he was about fifteen John said, "It must have been so cool. It must have been so cool when we were all together." I pushed my depression down and let my heart sting for my son. I felt such heartache for him and just listened to what he wanted to say.

Then there was the moment after the sports banquet in his high school gym. Long-stemmed roses were provided for the moms. All the mothers were lined up along the gym floor. My son grabbed two roses. He ran to me, gave me a hug and a kiss and a rose, and then ran over to Joan. He was sensitive, caring, considerate, and kind. I loved and love him so.

I was sitting with Joy at her kitchen table not too long ago. Now in her late thirties, she commented that she could hardly remember what it was like when we were all together. I was quiet. I was instantly sad. The comment triggered a *spontaneous and unexpected response.* (A concept I learned from Dr. Daniel Green in one of his many outstanding lectures.) After I left the house, I drove to the parkway on the way home. I parked on the side of the road and cried out loud in the car. I prayed that my mom and dad would not know I had been crying and that God would let me go through this and not be bitter. I prayed that the bitterness from long ago would not return. It was buried hurt. God answered my prayer.

I remembered the picture my daughter drew of me and Bob saying "I love you" to each other when she was little when we were still living as a family, shortly before we told the kids about the plan to divorce.

(As I sat on the porch considering the above accounts, I groaned and paused. This was also when I realized that Bob's affairs were probably at least back to back and maybe simultaneous. I rubbed my face, pulled back my hair, and moaned again. This business of climbing down the crevasse was disturbing and painful.)

Joan was there when we picked out the wedding dress for my Joy. It was so sad for me, so difficult. I was very happy for my beautiful young daughter. I adore her. She tried on a number of dresses. When she put on the dress that was simply *her*, I cried. The woman helping us at the bridal salon wrote down on her clipboard, "Mom cried." Then Joy and I had a crazy adventure together, racing down to Chicago to secure the dress after the store went bankrupt. (A huge smile crossed my face when I remembered that part.)

At another sports banquet, my son introduced us to his friends at the table. "This is my mom, and these are my parents."

I had to sell the house. I couldn't afford it any more. Being a single mom and working more than full-time hours, taking care of a house and yard was more than I could handle. There were many great memories there, but many painful ones as well. It would be good to be in an apartment that held new memories without Bob.

After Bob asked the Catholic Church to annul our twelve-year marriage with three children, my children stood up in Bob and Joan's wedding, of course. Before they were married, they lived together (off and on I guess) while the children were on visitation with Bob.

They had a condo in Arizona. For about fifteen years, they took my kids to Arizona for Thanksgiving, so I never spent Thanksgiving with my kids during that time. I let it go. I didn't want to put the kids in the middle and create a situation full of friction for them. I also sensed that this was a good time for their vacation from Bob's business standpoint. It probably worked quite well for them over the holiday. When they stopped going to Arizona for Thanksgiving and were back in town again at the holidays, Bob and Joan were adamant and insisted that the now-married Three would be at their house on Thanksgiving at X-o'-clock sharp. All those years, I had made it easy for them. I had even been fine celebrating Thanksgiving on another weekend. I had made a choice not to demand rights to have the kids every other Thanksgiving. But now, so many years later, they showed no respect for me or reciprocal appreciation. I was once again powerless to influence someone to care.

There are many situations where I decided to "take the slap" and not assert my rights. To make a stand would have triggered friction for my kids. To the extent I could keep them out of the middle of things, I would and I did. My friends kept track of the weeks I had the kids and would not even bother to ask me to get together on those weekends, because they knew how important my kids were to me.

One time I expressed my anger over how one of the kids had been treated. Bob came over to my house and shoved me around the kitchen table. I screamed at him to get out. He has never set foot in my home again.

I could describe many other stories besides these few I recorded in my journal during this grueling climb down the crevasse. The recollections are sad and very tiring, even exhausting. As I wrote in my journal, I often paused and moaned over the memories. And when I read the notes to put them into the computer, I felt tired of it all. I saw once again a situation where my feelings and well-being did not matter to my ex-husband. I could not influence him to care when we were married, and I know I can't now.

———————

I have found that when I have at last let myself be known and feel understood by someone who cares, the pain is lifted out and the memory of the offense is transformed and loses its sting.

———————

I had told the Three I was sorry for creating hurt in their lives. I had always thought they were happy at their dad's, and they were; but there were some difficulties I had not known about. I don't know if Bob and Joan ever apologized to my three children. This life was not of my children's choosing, not the best for them or what they would have preferred. Life became harder. Things hurt.

My pregnancies with my three precious gems were all very lonely. My husband abandoned, disregarded, and disrespected their mother, not protecting her or loving her as she deserved to be loved. This dynamic impacted their lives. I failed my children by not inserting myself into the situation and claiming my rights. My suppression and repression of self was not healthy for any of us.

Beth found the words for my resentment push down for so long: *We were not all together because of Bob's infidelity.* Resentment was uncovered. I claimed my right and God given empowerment to release that resentment. This is tough. My children belong to God. How good of God to let them into my life.

I am overjoyed, delighted, happy, and grateful for all the wonderful years I had and have with my children. I was and remain happiest when I am in their company.

NOT ALONE IN FEELING FLAWED, UNLOVABLE, AND LONELY

In September 2011, Gideon, my cat, ran away. My kids were all at their dad's for a wedding. My sister happened to call to see how I was doing;

we talked for a long time. She was, as always, loving; and now, knowing my story, she was also very understanding. (Jan and my brother were like much needed power bars that supplied essential energy for the climb.) We laughed at times. Jan recalled how her son talked about the late night assembly around the only phone available when we were up in Door County on vacation. He, too, remembered standing by the phone booth by the woods outside the ranger station and courageously fending off the attack of the mosquitos.

I did all that I could and much, much more, and I release myself from the idea that I didn't do enough. The situation was never mine to control. So now I have friends who know and understand. They saw the difficulties and the discouragement.

I realized how sad I was as I lifted weights at the Y. I guess I was feeling kind of depressed the last few weeks, especially today. And Gideon was still lost. I was sad and did not feel like getting together with anyone. I passed on joining family for ice cream. I wanted to pause.

I remembered when I felt unloved, and I felt lost from what I knew God to be. Gideon was lost, but never unloved or unwanted. I never stopped loving my lost cat; God never stopped loving the lost me. *Lord, do not let me be led astray from a sincere and pure devotion to you.*

When I think of speaking and writing so that God is lifted high, I feel supercharged and want to live on and on and on to serve God in this way. I want to live, live, live. What if I had only three years for this ministry? How could I be available in the fullest measure?

About six months into my journey of discovery and recovery, Beth prayed for a venue for me to speak and the imperative that I recognize the anointing for this ministry. She emphasized the importance that I act.

A few days later, I emailed my resignation as chaplain for the company where I had been serving. My last day would be November 14, 2011. I had valued and enjoyed my position as chaplain, but my downward climb demanded great energy and was time-consuming. Writing my story was richly compelling to me. I was required to follow this deep calling in order to be more fully available to serve.

Beth explained: *Your readers and your audience include those who need to confess the sins committed against them by their spouses and those who have committed the offenses. Both are concealed in suffocating shame; neither has a place of shelter or safety. Those who receive your story bear the burden of feeling that they are so flawed that no one can understand, and so they mustn't speak. You have been on both sides. You know how it feels: no longer lovable, sin too great to be shared, or sins against you make you feel so flawed. It is an incredible loneliness for both players in this drama.*

Jesus carried our shame. Sometimes we church people try to smear it back onto others or onto ourselves. Many know what it is like to be affected by infidelity, and most—if not all—are afraid to draw near to others and be known. I sure was. There is true guilt, and there are destructive consequences. Those on both sides of the crime often feel unlovable. They feel flawed and defective. They often withdraw into a suffocating loneliness or throw a huge part of themselves into the kind of deep crevasse I've been describing. The fear of being known can be excruciating. But God will forgive even this. He will remove the shame and will renew and restore. We feel the real shame, imposed shame, and also an imagined shame; and it is so awful that we are afraid to approach God's throne. To approach people in our network of friends and family is a dreaded nightmare. We are paralyzed in our shame and imagined defectiveness.

When people know they matter to God and he offers forgiveness to a repentant heart, it becomes safe to approach his throne room. When we lead with grace and compassion, we make it safe for people to share their stories and come to a place of forgiveness where God removes shame.

They can experience restoration. We can create an environment where people can heal.

Often, Christians who are feeling these kinds of shame feel they cannot safely go to the Christian community. People feel isolated, or even like outcasts. They feel shunned. They come out of the church building and community. This is not what God intends. We are to create a place for others to be heard, no blocking or barriers. People have already been violated; we are not to victimize them again. With other sins, we are not typically labeled personally flawed and defective. We need to deal with the despairing sense of defectiveness that imprisons people. They feel desperate—no, more than that. They feel hopeless. We need to help one another so that we do not deliver a message of defectiveness.

There is a next step made possible with God's generous provision of grace. It is reconciliation. Reconciliation is not a whim or a simple fancy that humankind came up with. It is a provision of divine design to restore relationship and bring healing, not to settle for a scab on the injuries. There can be a restoration, no more secrets kept, no more hurt concealed. It is made possible in the love and grace of God. It is God's desire that we are reconciled to one another. It is also his divine desire that we are personally reconciled with our authentic, broken and wounded self, so we can *be fully present.*

16

LEARNING IN ADVERSITY AND FINDING WISDOM IN AUTHENTICITY

ADVERSITY, AUTHENTICITY, ADVENT

How I regarded myself was undergoing a positive growth spurt when I was a junior and senior in high school. My self-esteem was fragile, but getting stronger. In my marriage I did not recognize the truth that I was being devalued, nor did I identify the accompanying emotions. It seemed that in order to recognize the reality of my degrading experience, I needed to reclaim my personal identity and realize my self-worth. So very quickly I lost my newly forming adolescent identity and assumed the id of *wife Mary*. This Mary had no voice, no rights, and was a very solitary, private identity filled with thoughts, but not known to herself. I was locked into an abusive situation. My wife-life was hyper focused on the relationship and was intent on getting back to the relationship as it was, one in which I was loved.

I discovered in therapy, that according to parts theory, you are the manager of your parts; but it's normal not to fully integrate all of them. We usually put out parts of ourselves to the world. It is a normal function of personality. But if you relate to *all* others with only parts of yourself, the only people who *could* really know you don't. Beth explained, "If your children never connect with the authentic you, they don't fully know you.

You are not fully known, and that adds to your loneliness. By managing your parts, you have perfected your role."

Beth said to put the following in my own words: "You are the happy cheerleader. You are a source of unconditional love and devotion. You don't use others or impose on them. You are a giver. You are an audience for their lives. You provide real encouragement, enabling confidence and inspiration for them to do great things. Your children then aspire to be like you. You are no muss, no fuss. You are not intrusive or depleting. All these years, you kept part of you secret, like a shadow, shoved away."

There was the day Katy got off the school bus and raced up to me as I sat sipping coffee on the patio and asked if my sad look was because of the divorce. I had said, "Yes, I am feeling pretty sad today." Beth told me that I was essentially saying to my daughter, "Yes, there's my shadow, but we're not going to talk about it."

Then there was the time I sustained a neck injury in a car accident, and my son said, "I never had a fragile mom before."

Beth explained, "You had a personal and a public persona. Your 'mother' persona was public; you excluded the 'sad' persona [your shadow]." She added, "These are two words I want you to write down: *congruent* and *authentic*. Your shadow wasn't congruent with your mother persona. To be authentic and integrated, the unwanted needs to be allowed out of the shadow to let your whole self be known. You need to let your children sometimes see you when you are not in the giving and inspirational role." I need to let them see the sad, the tired, the lonely me.

I truly do understand intimacy with Christ as a balm for loneliness. I do understand why it is often encouraged as a method of dealing with loneliness, but I know now it is not the whole method. Jesus was known to others, and I, too, must make all of myself known to at least one human other. Jesus had God in Gethsemane, but wanted his friends with him as well. My disconnected naiveté, unacquainted with the deeper adversity of the human experience, was not sufficient for Christian maturity. I needed to know human hardship, my own hardened heart, and to come face to face with my frailties, fallibility, and fallen condition.

On the live stage of adversity, with authentic and candid conversation rather than an artificial and contrived script, the real Mary could meet the real Jesus. It was important for me to know that I matter to Jesus, or it would be too terrifying to approach his holy presence. With all of me "above-board," I needed to know that he wanted me to join him at his table. On this real-life stage, being seated at the real table with continuing authentic and candid sharing of self would mark the advent of being fully known by others, allowing healing to take place and freedoms to take hold.

You aren't as lonely if you are true to who you really are: this statement is truthful and logical, actually. If I push away my real self or if I disregard my real self in any way, then my real self is alone. I have abandoned my true self in the past. Loneliness is the by-product of not being who I truly am.

I want you to see God in my story; I want you to see him working in your life story. I write this book so that others, too, might find affirmation, compassion, hope, release, relief, and freedom.

A PRISON IS A PRISON IS A PRISON

The morning of January 23, more than ten months since I began this life passage, the thought of a prison emerged from a much-traveled corridor of my mind. I pondered-What prison would be the most awful? One you choose to stay in or one you are forced to stay in? Which is most difficult? No one chooses oppression. Do we choose to stay? Where is the pain the greatest and the loss most extreme?

What kind of prison is the worst? One with iron bars whose prisoner has been accused, convicted, and sentenced for a crime he or she actually committed? Or when the prisoner is convicted and sentenced but is innocent? What if no reason at all is given for the imprisonment, yet the prisoner is left there and, in time, remembered by no one?

Is the worst prison a chamber of horror where a child is molested and raped in the permitted business of sex trafficking? Or when a child is molested and raped by one who claims to be an ambassador for Christ?

Is it the womb, which can offer protection and nourishment for an unborn child until delivery into the world, but becomes a prison where death is imminent when abortion has been chosen?

Is it the dark cell in a foreign nation where the prisoner of war is held captive? Is it the dark memory that relentlessly and mercilessly intrudes into the daily life of a war hero trying desperately to forget the horror and trauma of war? Is it the life of this war hero, wounded for our freedom, and now denied help by a nation that has forgotten her sacrifice?

Is it the so-called home of a person who is verbally beaten up day after day to the point of forgetting who he or she once was and any sense of self-worth or contributing value in this world? Is it the four walls of a house where the wife is beaten every weekend beyond facial and emotional recognition? Is it the four walls of a house where someone is abused physically, emotionally, or verbally and he or she is living in denial or in fear of telling anyone about it? Or where no one believes him or her when the truth is told? Or where the religion and/or politics claims such abuse is allowed?

Is it a place where someone chooses to stay in and devalues her- or himself by staying?

Is it the "land of the free and the home of the brave," where many races at one time or another—most for generation after generation after generation—were enslaved, abused, oppressed, and suppressed?

Is it within the walls of poverty and limited opportunity imposed by the greed and disregard of others?

Prison of Limited Opportunity for a Young Child in a School in Sudan December 2006

Is it within the walls of a poverty of one's own making?

Is it an illness that limits life and living in some way?

Is it a prison the individual chooses to stay in? Is it a prison where he or she has no choice to come or go? Is it a prison of his or her own making, or one that is imposed?

Is it a prison where someone is chained by an unexplainable propensity to do wrong, no matter how hard they seem to try not to? Is it a prison where a person is trapped by a felonious way of living modeled by elders and others around them?

Is it my fault? Is it your fault? Is it their fault? Whose fault is it? Does it matter?

Am I the victim? A collaborator? The perpetrator? Am I free to go, but paralyzed in my mind? Who has the key for my release?

Who has come to set the captives free?

A prison is any place a woman, man, or child is restricted in some way from developing and using their full created potential in

life and living, here on earth and in eternity. No matter what the prison is, no matter how we are held captive, we want to get out. We want to be set free.

Prison Isolation in Belize 2007

Beth said, "This is a depressing place." Yes, it was indeed.

Why did the concept of prison appear from around the corner? Was my memory of my marriage taking the shape of a prison? Had I felt trapped? If so, how? Things are confusing. Beth shared that usually, fear is at the root of confusion. Fear creates it. And prison is about fear. We often make a mistake and think that love is like a prison. We think staying is about love.

Could my fear be the fear to love or a fear to be known? Was it a fear of being rejected? I already had been rejected, but I denied it for years. I felt the anguish and the despair of rejection. I already hurt. Did I fear to face what it all meant? Was mine a fear of uncertainty? Fear of the unknown? (It couldn't be any worse than the known.) Was it a fear of disapproval by others? Was it fear of failure and the failure being known? Was it fear of abandonment? I already felt the abandonment. Was I afraid to get out?

Beth pointed out: "To stay for the wrong reason is a well-traveled place." So was it that I kept myself in prison for what I thought was love, but was actually fear? Confusing. I did not value myself and increased my devaluation. What I am figuring out here is that my prison wasn't about love. I did love someone, but remaining in a prison was not about that love. Staying is made to look like love, but it is only a layer of paint over the fear so that people (including myself) are distracted from seeing the fear.

(Oh. I was afraid of the truth. If I remained in this camouflaged prison, I could remain in denial of the truth. How sad was that? Eight months later I typed this revelation.)

"You demanded internally and intensely that Bob hang on to your relationship."

I realize now that he essentially—and quite dramatically—was saying, "No," by the way he was treating me.

"You were in shackles of fear, as strong as you are, as strong as you were."

I was living in denial of the truth; I was insisting that the truth be otherwise. I was afraid to be known; I was afraid of being rejected. I was afraid of not being loved. My fearful love kept me there. I escaped my prison walls through destructive measures. The walls came down, and a way out was made as my prison collapsed. *The door had never been locked.* It was fear that had locked me in. Beth pointed out how sad it is when we—and when others—won't accept the open door. We can climb out through the rubble or we can climb back in to be barricaded in again with fear.

I can now make decisions without fear in God's love and living in authenticity.

Now if I am rejected, I can face it differently and come out whole. I can make a decision in God's love without fear and unshackled by confusion. In the certainty of God's love, I can make my decision outside of fear. I am excited about living life without the depressing burden of these fears.

Beth helped me understand. "You needed to give love to Bob. His infidelity was saying, 'I don't need you. You don't have what I want.'" She continued, "'You're everything I want; I need you' is what Bob couldn't give. What he couldn't give you, he gave you through the children. Bob couldn't give his love to you, but gave you three children to whom you could give and receive love. God looked ahead for gifts and blessings. It is very rare when there are two working sides, parent and children. It is rare that you have a beautiful reciprocal relationship with all three children."

An old friend of mine said to me, "How did you get in such an enviable position of being able to say that your children are your best friends?" Yes, God was so very generous to me.

"You lost yourself in your kids," Beth commented. "Coping, for you, was to lose yourself in your kids. What did you get out of loving so well? It also soothed you in some way. Mothering well was calming for you. Your children needed you. What you put in, you got back. It was an antidote for him. It was a perfect solution for how you give love." Beth then asked, "Could you have been the mother you were if you had remained married to Bob?"

Right away, I had answered no. I would have become more and more depleted. I would not have been fully present in the lives of my children. I would have been compelled to please Bob and would have remained fearful of not pleasing him. My destructive marriage would have sabotaged my ability to be devoted to and for my Joy, Katy, and John. My husband's person and personality would have continued to suffocate me and oppress me. I had forfeited so much of myself to survive in a relationship with Bob. My children would not have known the strong mother I am. I am happiest when getting together with family and extended family.

Beth had helped me to see how my affair had broken down walls and made a way to climb out of what was broken and harmful—not only my husband's fulfilled promise to be unfaithful, but also my own frailty and sin, which I see in full color now. God used the affair and my betrayal of him similarly to the way he used Peter's drama of betrayal. When I was young, I would boldly claim that I would stand strong, yet in high school my personal fortitude was cracked; my frailty was exposed. As ugly as my affair was, as ugly as my denial of God was, as horrible as Peter's denial of Christ was, God used it for Peter, and God used my affair and my betrayal of him to make things clear to me. It exposed my capacity for sin and to forfeit myself, one who was created in God's image; and it made known my capacity to deny my creator.

Why, why, why this personal weak spot, my sin nature and choices spiraling out of control? It was not the bitterness I told God I did not want anymore many years ago: *I don't want to be like this anymore.* He had released me from that. It was an even deeper issue. I had held onto the pain because I never brought it to light and because holding on to the pain of the memory tags something of great value to me. I loved Bob and gave my all to him, which never was enough. It meant nothing to him.

I can now take that love spent and the tears shed and ask God to mingle them with his precious and pure blood and tears so it is made holy in my offering to him, my Lord, for his purposes. For this, too, all the sin and ugly done on my part, all the love spent, God can and did use for his kingdom purposes. All has been woven into his eternal plan, his perfect will and kind intentions, his perfect pleasure. The pain, the sin, the loss—all was redeemed through the mystery of the Cross. All of my authentic parts are not always pretty. All the parts of me, my pain, my sin, my betrayal, and my loss: all is redeemed through the Cross.

SHARING FRESH SUSHI AND NEW WISDOM

I like sushi and recently discovered a lovely and classy restaurant with marvelous chefs. I made a reservation for my daughter, her husband, and me one evening. When we arrived, it was quaint and welcoming to see a table had been prepared with three place settings and three menus standing upright.

We first requested water and green tea, and then shared a seaweed salad. The conversation was as fine as the serving of delicacies. Each of us shared updates of what was going on in our stories at that time. I shared where I was at in my journey and my writing.

I was sharing my learning that had broken ground and blossomed in my recent sessions with Beth. The blossoms were magnificent and now were bearing fruit. I shared how Beth's teaching and guidance helped me comprehend still more about forgiveness and about how we can be guided and also guide others through the process. A first step for me was when I ran out of myself and didn't want to be as I was anymore, and I knew I needed Jesus Christ and his offering of forgiveness and freedom. This fundamental forgiveness was monumental and essential. Nothing has been the same since. And now, at this place in my life, I had been required to go deeper still.

Discerning why I had hung onto the pain was an emancipating revelation. Although I held the pain far below the surface of things and did not think on it anymore, it was not dormant. Remember, buried emotions are never inactive. The pain represented something of great value. It embodied the unconditional investment of my love, and me. It was emblematic of my sacrifice. And now I realized in the hands of God it would reap a harvest of good. I was enabled to surrender this gift to God. When I release it to God as a broken and spilled-out offering, he makes it all worthwhile. He will reap the harvest. Nothing will be lost or wasted. I was required to go deeper and deeper into the crevasse, lifting the past up into the light by sharing my story, sharing the pain. The whole of it all is exposed, validated, accepted and understood; permitting release that was before hindered.

My sushi sharers commented, "You transcended it."

One of them asked, "What if they said they were sorry?" I told the raw salmon lovers that if it were said in an apparently trite, flippant, sarcastic or empty way; it would not offer healing but rather once again invalidate and discredit the injury. Bob needs to hear my story, for to ignore, nullify, disregard, or outright deny the depth of it all would just add more injury. If he listened to it, he would be demonstrating an effort of sincerity.

Apart from any sign of remorse, release and forgiveness is made possible in God, who is the very source of love and the divine benefactor of forgiveness.

I likened the tug of war between holding onto pain and being able to release it to the harsh reality of the persecution of African Americans for generation upon generation. People may hang onto their pain in all its hideousness, because it represents something of great value. And yes, the injuries may be reoccurring and the damage of the past so severe. When I returned to college and studied intercultural communication, I was just becoming aware of the suppression and oppression I experienced in my marriage and how I was devalued. To some small degree, I began to identify with my fellow Americans and came to a heart-wrenching, barrier-breaking realization. During a lecture on the African American experience, as I felt a growing awful and sickening heaviness; I unintentionally said out loud, "We suppressed an entire race."

"What was that?" the professor had asked. I repeated myself, now deliberately out loud, "We suppressed an entire race."

God have mercy. We oppressed an entire race for centuries. Dehumanizing human beings is an affront to the God who made them. God have mercy. We murdered, lynched, and brutalized women, men, and children. God have mercy. We scorned, shamed, and sinned against fellow human beings. God forgive us. For us to listen to the heart cry of African Americans (and Native Americans), to exhibit understanding of the awfulness of it all, and to get on our knees to say we are sorry, would help healing happen and would make a way for lateral forgiveness: one human being for another, only made possible by heaven's horizontal cross.

Now then, here is another analogy for us to embrace and apply. The cross of Christ had a vertical beam and a horizontal crossbeam. Some think of the horizontal beam as a bridge over the great divide between sinful humanity and a holy, holy, holy God and the redemption and rescue made possible by the life, death, and resurrection of Jesus Christ. The horizontal crossbeam of the cross of Christ can also represent the intentions of God that the life, death, and resurrection of Christ also provide a way and an expectation for us to say, "I am sorry," to seek and offer forgiveness to one another.

I am convinced that the only thing that can bring healing is God's gift of redemption, provided for us through the life, death, and resurrection of Jesus Christ. By his wounds, we can be healed of our sins and rescued from our guilt, our shame, and our disgrace.

The availability of redemption, however, does not release a perpetrator—ourselves included—from acknowledging our wrongdoing, knowing the full disclosure of the effects of our abuse, and then, in that precious place to exhibit some comprehension of the injury we caused. We must still offer confession to the person, people, or people group we have wounded. It is a precious place for a woman, man, or child who was mistreated and who has had their well-being endangered. It is a precious place, for it was only made available by the purchase price of the spilled blood of Jesus. It is a precious place because a human being's worth is validated; it is a precious place because confession can help us all heal.

When I realize—when *you* realize—that you matter to God and that he cares about you, it becomes safe to approach the throne of a holy, holy, holy God and tell him, "I am sorry. I hurt you and others, I sinned against you, and I am sorry. Forgive me." When we confess our sins, he is faithful to forgive them in his grace and by the life of Jesus, his death on the cross, and his resurrection to new life. In this dynamic process of confession, we experience a release from guilt and shame, a healing, and a renewal, pregnant with a new hope and new energy and new life.

In a state of having received forgiveness from God, we are equipped with a capacity to confess to those we have offended. To do so helps stop their bleeding.

To say we are sorry to those we have injured is a powerful step that moves us closer to restoration, reconciliation, and healing. To withhold these words may indeed add more than one brick to a wall that already stands in the way of someone turning to Christ. God can still break through, but if we are on in his team, why create a stumbling block on someone's long journey to a relationship with God? He requires us to confess our wrongdoing to those we have injured.

Search my heart, Lord. Holy Spirit show me and lead me to confess to anyone I have offended. Bring to heart and mind an understanding of my offense and lead me to confession. Search my heart and replace my pride with humility, replace my ignorance and coldness with awareness and informed understanding. Give me humble courage and the wisdom required for me to say the words "I am sorry." Change whatever needs changing in my heart and mind that I may bring you honor and remove any barrier I have left standing between this individual, this group, and recovery, or even a barrier between them and a relationship with you. Prepare their heart to receive my confession.

I believe this is a rare thing, this act of confession. It is a discipline that lacks practice. We make excuses; we cover up. We color over. We may deny our wrongdoing all together. We might tell someone to just get over it. Perhaps someone has said that to us.

God- I give you, then, my loneliness, my sadness, my heartache, my shame, my grief, and my frailty. Fill me, Lord, with your love, your joy, your peace, your contentment, your strength, your power to overcome, your goodness, your truth, your honesty, your beauty, and your great grace. I want to be fully devoted to you above all else. In your name and in your mercy, Lord, may I write this book for your honor. I desire to see, feel, and know that I do love you far more deeply than words can ever say. (Jesus showed me that feeling. I felt him draw near. I do love him. I always will.)

This is a truth to ponder: God works out everything in conformity with the purpose of his will and with his incomparable great power. Consider these beautiful words of truth and encouragement from the Bible: *It's in Christ that we find out who we are and what we are living for. Long before we first heard of Christ and got our hopes up, he had his eye on us, had designs on us for glorious living, part of the overall purpose he is working out in everything and everyone. (Ephesians I, The Message)*

Emancipation from the past, from holding on to the pain, from wrong-being and wrongdoing, is made available to us all.

The miracle of forgiveness is not complete without repentance. To act as if we need not say we are sorry to God or to others is a mockery. Forgiveness is a relational reaction that requires the presence of the heartfelt words, "I am sorry." Oxygen alone does not make water. Hydrogen alone does not turn into water. H2O requires both hydrogen and oxygen. The combination of divinely provided forgiveness and divinely enabled repentance is living water, a refreshing and life-giving drink.

Forgiveness is made ready for us. Remember, Jesus stands at the door. He has his right hand on the doorknob. He has turned the doorknob so that the latch is released. Forgiveness is at the door. With a desire to receive God's forgiveness, breathe in his love and his offering and exhale your humble repentance. The door cracks open as you exhale and forgiveness rushes in. Let forgiveness rush in. Let forgiveness rush in. Let forgiveness rush in.

17
COMPASSION

CONSIDER AND CLAIM THE COMPASSION OF CHRIST

Drop the stone and pick up grace!

Compassion does not make a wrong right.

Not condemning does not mean condoning.

We are called to walk with people through despair. Often, we would rather offer solutions and resolutions. Instead, we are to pull up a chair and listen to their stories. Care enough to listen, listen enough to understand; understand enough to care, and continue to listen. Your presence is needed and it is a gift; your imposition of solutions is not requested.

Beth explained, "Feeling the need to remind and persuade is often a cloak covering condemnation and depicts people often having insecurity with grace. There is no place for persuasion when we do not understand or even know the story. Persuasion can strike a lethal blow."

The church community is often quick to say, "Divorce is not an option." Whether right or wrong, it is there for one to choose or not to choose. The quick, draw-from-the-hip responses when hearts are already breaking can be deadly. Our rapid fire can miss the mark and trigger alienation from the church family. It is important, even critical, to create a place in our church heart to be kindhearted and allow listening and caring, to be compassionate and accepting of people who are hurting.

Beth's shared her thoughts related to Last Days: *In the end times, "the love of most grows cold." (Matthew 24: 12 Because of the increase of wickedness, the love of most will grow cold.) Why will the love of most grow cold? As people, we are tested in the end times. God has been restraining evil. In the end times, evil will be let loose on earth. There will likely be more and more divorce. As believers are tested, we will feel a lack of empathy and compassion from the church; people will lose faith when love and hope faints, fails, or falls. The church may put up walls. (Alienating others in this way is another failure of church unity.) People may leave the faith out of hurt and disillusionment. If those who are hurting and broken feel alienated at their most vulnerable and painful time, the church can become irrelevant for them. How will the body of the church perceive the helping process? Will the church be a place for people to heal when they are falling?*

In the book of Revelation, we read how the church of Ephesus did indeed fulfill this prophecy of Jesus quoted above: *You have persevered and endured hardships for my name, and have not grown weary. Yet I hold this against you: You have forsaken your first love.* (Revelation 2:3-4)

In his commentary on Revelation, theologian Grant Osborne writes, "The problem of the Ephesians is the abandonment of their first love." (p. 115) He goes on to explain that "first love" does not mean a primary love but rather the love the people of the church in Ephesus had at first. Osborne states that the second generation of the church in Ephesus lauded orthodoxy above loving God and neighbor. "They had lost the first flush of enthusiasm and excitement in their Christian life and settled into a cold orthodoxy with more surface strength than depth." (p. 115) Their love had grown cold. It appears that the church's severe realities of persecution, its battle against false teachers, and its consuming determination to fight against heretical instruction so very prevalent in that time, essentially drained the people of the church of love for one another. Osborne put it this way:

It is clear that the Ephesians loved truth more than they loved God or one another. This does not mean that they were not believers or that they had no love at all, for the commendations of verses 2-3 would be impossible in that case. Rather, their early love had grown cold and been replaced with a harsh zeal for orthodoxy. (p. 116)

As Christians in 2012, we are not exempt from the potential to abandon our first love or from alienating those who are seeking God from a place of pain. We, too, can betray our love and compassion for others in the name of religious requirements, even perfection. *God, please forgive me for when I have abandoned love for you and others. God help me. God help us for I have seen it in my heart and actions and in the actions of others. And it is ugly.*

The church of Jesus Christ must stand firm in holding out Christ's offer of love, hope, and unmerited grace. The love of Christ unites us. We are all sinners. We are all saved by costly grace. When we approach the throne of a holy, holy, holy God, it helps to know that we matter to him. We must take great care not to condemn people but to hold out hope and the promise of redemption and restoration offered by Jesus. We must not restrict the hand of God.

The compassion of God is his persistent, perpetual, and plentiful kindness, patiently poured out for needy and miserable women, men, and children who are in a mess and who mess things up on a regular basis.

God is the only one who can help us. Grace is required to help sinners; compassion is needed to extend persistent, perpetual, plentiful, and tender kindness to despicable, needy, and frail people. God, whose qualities and attributes include grace and compassion, is the endless reservoir that supplies our capacity to extend compassion to others.

In truth, the best way to define, explain, and clarify the compassion of God is to see what it looks like.

ESSENTIAL COMPASSION

Jesus had been falsely accused, brutally beaten, tortured, and crucified. Some say it was murder. On the evening of the first day of the week, after Jesus had risen from the dead, he appeared to his disciples who were huddled together in a locked room. "Peace be with you," Jesus said. Then it is written, *Now Thomas called Didymus, one of the Twelve, was not with the disciples when Jesus came. So the other disciples told him, 'We have seen the Lord!'* (John 20:24-25 NIV)

Can you just imagine the excitement of the disciples? They had known Thomas for the past three years and had walked alongside one another, talking for hours on end. It was an intimate band of men called together, sharing, caring, struggling, growing closer to Jesus and to each other. They must have known each other well. How desperately they must have wanted to share what they had seen, the joy they now knew. Did they all talk at once? They must have been so intense and passionate about it all, yet Thomas responded to their testimony by adamantly refusing to believe without proof. He wanted dramatic evidence to cancel doubt before he would believe. (John 20: 25 NIV) He seemed to be immovable. *But he said to them, 'Unless I see the nail marks in his hands and put my finger where the nails were, and put my hand into his side, I will not believe it.'* (John 20:25 NIV)

Thomas is often labeled "doubting Thomas," but the epithet really is limiting and not fair-minded. He would have followed Jesus anywhere, whether it was dangerous or not. Courageous Thomas would have suited him just as well. Now, Thomas had seen Jesus taken in the night, beaten, abused, and crucified. Having witnessed Lazarus, a friend of Jesus, raised from the dead was no consolation for him now. Jesus alive? Was it too hard to swallow? Too good to be true? Too impossible to imagine? Too risky to believe?

It is hard to believe the unbelievable when you are discouraged, when you have been cruelly disappointed, when the fear of disappointment again runs deep, deeper than human testimony can penetrate. It is hard to believe in heaven when you are standing in a world of pain. These are the people God shows compassion to: people in a world of disappointment, confusion, and hurt. People who have run out of hope. They have been disappointed in life before and don't want to risk it again. They are pained with guilt, distressed by shame, and can't believe the story, while aching for it to be true.

It is to hurting hearts such as this that Jesus offers compassion. *A week later, his disciples were in the house again, and Thomas was with them. Though the doors were locked, Jesus came and stood among them and said, 'Peace be with you!' (John 20:26)* I wonder if the disciples had been trying to convince Thomas all week long. I wonder if his heart had begun to soften—or was he just as reluctant to believe? That Sunday night, they were frightened and behind locked doors, not knowing what to expect, yet knowing they were in danger by meeting together. When Jesus arrived, had they been arguing or praying? Were they trying to sort things out? Deciding what to do next? Encouraging one another? Tired, confused? Trying to convince Thomas? Wondering if Jesus would show up again?

Can you imagine the face of Thomas when Jesus appeared? When he showed up behind locked doors? When Jesus repeated what Thomas had said a week earlier when he hadn't even been there to hear it? Jesus knew the heart of Thomas, understood his pain, and met him where he was at. He showed Thomas the evidence he needed. Jesus loved Thomas. Thomas mattered to Jesus. It is almost as if this was a special appearance just for the sake of Thomas.

We know it was a special appearance for all who are in need of hope, all who want to believe. It would have been quite amazing to see the face of Christ as he lovingly revealed himself to Thomas. What divine pleasure must show on the face of Jesus—to show up and reveal himself to a wounded, broken, and hurting heart and say, "It is me. I am here. I am here with you and you matter to me. Believe and have hope in this life now and hope for eternal life."

Moments of miracles of radical compassion such as this must delight Jesus. "Pick up your mat and walk! Lazarus, come out!" Appearing to Mary at the tomb, "Mary!" And now, "Stop doubting and believe!" Healing the sick, raising people from the dead, mending broken hearts, and changing lives in the here and now and for all eternity: what divine pleasure that must be for Jesus.

Jesus's essential compassion reminds us not to give up on those who are hurting and discouraged. The mission of Jesus is to seek and save the lost, the hurting, and the oppressed. His ardent compassion is like a banner that boldly claims, *"You, dear one, matter to me and to my father."* When you are hurting, when you are feeling guilty and sin burdened, when you know you have messed up, it helps to hear that you matter to God. To know he loves you makes it safe to approach the throne of compassion and grace. In his abounding compassion, he makes a special appearance to us.

Jesus showed up behind locked doors and stood among those hiding from the awfulness of the world. He revealed the truth about himself to Thomas. *'Put your finger here; see my hands. Reach out your hand and put it into my side. Stop doubting and believe.' Thomas said to him, 'My Lord and my God.' (John 20: 27-28)*

Jesus shows up and lives change direction. Jesus knew and was sensitive to the heart of Thomas and showed him compassion. The zealous compassion of Christ let loose in a hurting world is a very powerful force. We do not know the circumstances of someone's hurt, shame, guilt, discouragement, or hopelessness. We have to stop and listen to someone's story and consider and become the compassion of Christ.

A PERMISSION SLIP

"Some people want to wave the permission slip of adultery as a go-ahead for divorce. Why didn't you feel like you had a permission slip?" asked Beth.

"Your loyalty was not based on rules and regulations. Your loyalty was based on love, no matter how many times you forgave. No matter how many times he had affairs, you forgave. You were not able to leave, for it would be a failure of love to do so. It would mean you gave up and love failed. True love, it doesn't give up. Unconditional, unselfish love stays. And to do otherwise is to fail in your commitment. Even though you had a 'permission slip,' it was still as big of a failure for you."

My experience when I lived on Beloit Road was the darkest place for me. I mean, they all were tough, but there, things were so dark. I remembered when my Joy was asleep in her crib, and I said to myself, "I won't have Bob with me until we are old and sitting side by side in rocking chairs." And then, as I continued to ponder this forecast I added, "Oh, no, maybe I still won't have Bob with me. I will still be alone." It was a realization of future hopelessness in my marriage to Bob. My continuing commitment to love—a love that had no return—was indeed loving my husband into a future that had no promise.

Beth added, "There was no hope for you to be heard. No hope to be heard in a marriage, for whatever reason—whether an affair or another mode of invalidation—is no hope. No hope is no hope."

Is it okay to continue in a relationship when you are diminished, when you have no hope and no validation, are not heard and not understood? When the commitment has been undermined? When love and respect were divorced from the marriage a long time ago? When *cherish* was a word mentioned at the altar but never put into practice? When you cannot thrive and develop your full, God-given potential? The covenant was broken before a divorce on paper was even considered.

Too quickly we lead with correction when a breaking heart calls for compassion. So often we want to fix when someone needs a shoulder to cry on. We are at the ready to raise the hammer and take out the sin with one swift blow when someone has beaten themselves up already; what they need is a lifeline to pull them out of the pit they already know they are in. Most people are already aware of the sin predicament in a broken marriage relationship. Mind, heart, and spirit are already crumbling beneath the weights of sorrow and woundedness, sin and shame, guilt and failure, loss and grief. Anger, brokenness, and despair make their presence known.

First, consider, claim, and extend the compassion of Christ. *Listen to their stories; learn where they have been and where they are now before you even think you can tell them where they should be going.* Often the people bombarding the hurting with advising, judging and condemning statements have not really been engaged with or attentive to those they are trying to advise. Listen to their stories and hear their hearts' cry. Many times when we give reminders, advice, or solutions, we are essentially judging and condemning. Take care. Hear their stories, and only then minister hope where there is great sorrow.

Jesus will not break a bruised reed, nor should we. *A bruised reed he will not break, and a faintly burning wick he will not quench. (Isaiah 42:3 ESV)*

A memory rushed in from years and years before, the first time I ventured to attend a singles retreat. A lay minister in one session started out saying, "Today, people aren't willing to work through the hard stuff. They are too quick to give up...*yada, yada, yada.*" I don't think I walked out of the room, but I thought about it. "Does he have any idea of the awfulness and pain people go through and how deadly it is to stay?"

Don't lead with the sledgehammer. Reach out with your hand! Let's not raise the hammer of an accuser until we have listened to the testimony of one still reeling from the pounding of an abuser. As family and friends, as mothers and fathers, as brothers and sisters, may we all try to keep our hearts safe for them to return to. God keeps his heart safe for us to return to on all occasions. Most people in a broken marriage feel they have not been heard, let alone understood. And life is not safe.

Remember that you were at that time separated from Christ, alienated from the commonwealth of Israel and strangers to the covenants of promise, having no hope and without God in the world. But now in Christ Jesus you who were once far off have been brought near by the blood of Christ. (Ephesians 2:12–13)

I remember where I came from and the sin and the sinning I am still capable of. By grace I have been saved, and by grace I make it through each day. It was grace that brought me near to God.

Praise be to the God and Father or our Lord Jesus Christ, the Father of compassion and the God of all comfort, who comforts us in all our troubles, so that we can comfort those in any trouble with the comfort we ourselves have received from God. For just as the sufferings of Christ flow over into our lives, through Christ our comfort overflows. (2 Corinthians 1:3–5 NIV)

This is one of the grand plans of God unveiled: We can comfort those who are hurting, because we have known the comfort of God in our own lives.

Jesus is called the Lamb of God. The only time he describes himself in the Bible, the two words he chooses are *gentle* and *humble*. That says a lot about the high regard God has for gentleness and humility. *Come to me, all you who are weary and burdened, and I will give you rest. Take my yoke upon you and learn from me, for I am gentle and humble in heart, and you will find rest for your souls. (Matthew 11:28–29 NIV)*

God is the one who supplies us with endurance and encouragement. They are God's gifts to us. He is the God of hope that allows us to overflow with hope. (Romans 15:1–13 NIV)

I have been the recipient of God's grace and compassion. He has most definitely outfitted me with endurance and encouragement for the downward climb. I have known his kindness, gentleness, and humility in my life. In him I have found hope, a hope that overflows. My great and divine Benefactor has graciously and generously provided me with grand benefits, and I am to follow his lead. Thank Goodness! He will help me in doing so.

The arduous process of uncovering, identifying, and understanding our emotions is made even more complicated by the sometimes deafening clamor of *should do* and *should not do*, *should be* and *should not be*, *should say* and *should not say*, *should stop* and *should start*, *should remember* and *should forget*—and all in the past, present, and future tenses. It is a time of lunacy and craziness. Give it a rest. Give it grace. Give it compassion. Give a listening ear and a receptive heart. Be gentle and humble.

18

LOOKING CLOSELY AT THE LEAVES ON THE GROUND

Some people would say I am crazy when I say Wisconsin has great weather; others would agree that it does. I appreciate variety of the seasons. Often, winters are harsh and the snow is deep; spring sometimes slips in and out and we feel as if we almost missed it. Each season has its unique loveliness and offerings. Wisconsin autumns, for example, are quite spectacular.

The leaves of fall are one of the splendors of Wisconsin. Look up, and the trees are adorned with a multitude of colors. Green and gold are very popular. Yes, Green Bay Packer colors were surely God's idea. On early morning walks with Boaz, I would enjoy the trees lining the neighborhood streets that sported the brilliant gold and contrasting greens that lingered there.

One autumn, a few fallen leaves caught my eye. Walk after walk, I found myself looking down rather than up. Now I saw pinks and purples and shades of maroon, reds and browns and burnished black, pewter gray and silver tones. Ah, I found a perfect maple leaf with perfect points and form, a leaf still glossy from a light evening rain and highlighted with a shimmer cast by the morning sun. I picked it up by the slender, brown-black stem and rolled and twirled it in my fingers. Then I saw another.

I could make a pretty picture arrangement with some of these gathered leaves. I would press them between the pages of a book and let them dry.

Each morning I now found myself looking down on the ground noticing the leaves, the many, many leaves, lying there. Some were perfectly shaped, typically a requirement for selection by one who gathers leaves. Others seemed not quite so perfect, yet eye-catching and unique. Some had decorative blotches or tiny tears or leaf blemishes; some retained their original color. I found young, green leaves torn from their branches by gusts of wind or pummeling rain. I would find a leaf similar to one I had already chosen, but it would have different shades of color and singularly special markings. One maple leaf was unusually large—as large as a dinner plate. The holes and tears and sections of brittle, brown edging gave one large green leaf the look of lace. I imagined how distinctly lovely it would be in my changing and developing collage of leaves. Leaves from the same tree were not identical one to the other. Some were soft and young in color, others dry and brittle and a faded brown. When I looked up, I could see older leaves still attached to branches while younger ones had fallen to the ground seemingly prematurely. On another morning, leaves on the ground were frosted with an icing of morning dew; some leaves were pasted one to another.

I noticed a pretty and waxy oak leaf with perfectly punctured, elliptically shaped *hole*s, four or five or so. I wondered how they got there. Another morning, I noticed another oak leaf with four or five or maybe six oval fungus-like drops attached to its surface. I lifted one off—and there was a perfectly punctured, elliptically shaped hole. I don't yet know or understand the cause, nature, or name of the fungus, nor what the notable remaining markings might be called; but it all created a unique design. It was a design I had not seen before I began to look more closely at the lovely and unique leaves on the ground.

I can imagine God appreciating and valuing the beauty of each of us just like this. He creates a collage of the imprint of our images in his heart. Whether one still hangs on the tree or is on the ground really doesn't make much difference when you are as tall as God is.

The intricate and involved edging etched over the seasons of her life is lovely. The complex lacework is intriguing, exquisite, and experience-refined. A remarkable design is notable now from the imprints left by life's afflictions. The pale shades of faded color are in fact pleasing and distinctive and tell the story of life lived wholeheartedly. The bright and vibrant enduring colors have their own matchless message of the innate richness of one created in the image of her Maker. The shimmer still lingers from the tears of divinity that splashed and then revived her at times of wounding, brokenness, failure, and loss.

If you look carefully, you realize that there is nothing you would cover up or trim away. If you cover up the dark spots, you would block the shimmering gold threads where her weakness encountered grace. You realize that you must not cut out the imprints from harsh human encounters that at first make the viewer gasp. You discover that when you hold the image up to the light there is a glow there, becoming more and more brilliant, even radiant. This is the scarring revealed to other human hearts, to be handled with compassion. This is the dark bruising touched by the light of the world and used by the All-Knowing to make her gentler and stronger, more humble and far wiser, more human, and more like Jesus.

Every experience, each encounter, becomes a shaping contributor to the final piece. Erasing parts of her past and/or the people in it erases segments of the chapters in her story. We erase a part that takes her from there to here and from then to now. To trim away any part would be to subtract from the whole. It would disfigure rather than repair.

I see now and value too much of who I am and what I have been becoming to erase any part of the appearing design. God and I put way too much effort into this outstanding creation. Did you ever notice how small the word "I" looks next to the word "God?" (Yes, he gets all the credit. Including me in on the plan was his gracious idea.) And so many people have impacted who I am and what I am becoming. I have met and known so many great and wonderful people. It's amazing. My life and my living have been far richer because of the friendships I have known, the people I have worked with, the family I treasure, the people I have met from other nations and cultures. The number of people that I might recall with frustration or hurt is a small number in comparison. And to top that, what those few meant for harm, God used for good. The good, the bad, and the ugly were all included in the developing design of who I am, including my personal good, bad, and ugly. My tenacity is more tenacious, applied wisely and made usable by God. My stubbornness is steadfast love made humble, strong and rich. My knowledge is broader, my wisdom sharper. It was in those tough passages and the return to the dangerous crevasse that I learned more about me even as I learned more about God.

I would never go through my twenties again. In fact, quite a few years ago, I said if I had to go through my twenties again, I would rather not ever have lived.

The learning God let happen in my mess-making and brokenness added much good to my life. In his sovereign design and handle on things, God shaped me through what he allowed to happen in my life. He tended to my development, redeemed my life, and worked it all out in spite of me because he loves me. He is able, and he is an overcoming God.

I recently shared a story of a good friend who was traveling through hurting places. Beth encouraged me to communicate that this friend is still moral and virtuous and kind and good, in fact quite exceptional—to say to my friend that "This failure does not make you someone else."

I think this is an important truth to ponder in regard to ourselves and in regard to others.

Yes, I had entertained fear in sharing my hidden self. When I did take off the masks, I found out how doing so allows others to stop their charades, too. Being personally authentic creates a safer place for others to be authentic. We become stronger and more complete. We realize we are not living in an unending circus parade; we are on a life journey that is not always easy—in fact, probably never easy.

When I finally shared these long-lost parts of me, I felt better about myself: stronger and more complete. How can we ever feel complete if we deny parts of ourselves? Doesn't it just drive you nuts when you work hard on a thousand-piece jigsaw puzzle only to find the last few pieces are missing? How crazy, then, for us to deliberately bury the pieces that complete who we are.

19

WHAT DO WE DO WITH THE PAST?

MORE LEARNING ON FORGIVENESS

After reaching the extreme places of the crevasse, the guidance, wisdom, and insights from Beth helped me move to another level in the process of forgiveness. I did fundamentally forgive years ago, and that was a divinely remarkable step in the process. Now, as I went deeper into things of the past, there were injuries and offenses that I had buried with all the linked emotions. These now-unearthed offenses and how they affected me needed to be realized, understood, released, and forgiveness offered.

In addition I no longer needed to hang onto the pain that I harbored for so long (or the pain recently excavated) to give my love value in light of my former husband's disregard for it. I claimed that my love was not wasted, but rather esteemed in the eyes of God who is the origin of all love. He will reap the harvest.

I thought my ex-husband would respond with remorse in light of a number of recent situations. I truly thought he would demonstrate understanding and compassion for deeply loved and cherished friends in difficult circumstances. I was wrong. He chose judgment and condemnation as his response. I would say he withheld his love. And now, with twisted and disturbing irony, his wife also judged and condemned loved ones in desperate marital situations and in circumstances where divorce was chosen. We, who have been shown great grace and monumental mercy for our own outrageous sin, must likewise be merciful. How dare we do otherwise? How dare we? We need to consider and take to heart the parable Jesus told of the unmerciful servant who was forgiven a great debt and then refused to show that same mercy to another. (Matthew 18:21-35)

At this time of the final editing of the manuscript, I grieved with those who were already hurting and then faced with their condemnation. To treat others in such a way was *Ephesianistic,* narcissistic, and perverse. Nothing I could say or do would change their actions toward others or toward me. What I could do that made a difference was to love and support those who were hurt by their actions, and to pray for them and with them. In and with prayer for gentleness, humility, and wisdom; I could care enough to listen, listen enough to understand, and understand enough to continue to listen.

Foolishly I thought these situations might even prompt my former husband to step forward and say, "I am sorry, Mary." But no is no is no is no. This was like a new injury. I recognized new feelings of depression and other ways the current situations affected me. Now I could name and understand the anger and other accompanying emotions because I had worked *through* my past. Identifying and accepting anger and acknowledging the underlying message made a crucial difference for me. I did not deny my anger and allow erosion of a positive appraisal of who I am. Something was wrong. I should not have been treated in such- and- such a way. Others should not have been treated in such- and -such a way.

Yes. Yes! I know that I needed to be taken to the edge of the crevasse and loved and encouraged and guided as I began *the downward climb.* I believe that those who exhibit narcissistic characteristics as they move in relationships also need to be taken to the edge and loved and encouraged and guided in order to begin the downward climb. It's all great grace. I pray this opportunity will happen in the lives of Bob and his wife so they too can let go of pain, release the shame, and discover new freedom in authenticity.

I share this brief snapshot about more of the dynamics of forgiveness in order to illustrate how there will be reminders of the past and there may be reoccurrence of the injury, a related offense, or new circumstances that hurt. The words I-am-sorry will not likely be expressed. You and I need to make a decision to forgive again. It is wise to share the experience with a trusted friend who can listen to the story and provide support.

Having a greater understanding of this process of forgiveness, I can decide not to hang onto anything. I do not need recognition or validation from those who caused the injury. My love given was made possible through and only because of God. I lay it all at the altar again and he will reap the harvest. I have realized the new injury and I understand its effect on me; I release it and extend forgiveness. God has shown me great grace and infinite mercies. Day by day, moment to moment I desperately need his love and forgiveness. I need his strength. So help me God, my hand will remain turned on the doorknob on the door of forgiveness.

The Open Door?

Welcome! Welcome, Sinner!
We welcome you inside.
Come in from the cold!
Come in from the bitter world outside!
We welcome you in Jesus' name.
From this moment and forever more,
Nothing, no nothing will ever be the same.
To you, yes you, we offer the open door.
But you, you there in the time worn pew–
Yes, you, it is you we are talking to.
You have disregarded the rule made plain.
No clearer could it be.

We must tell you now to take your leave.
Go away, far away, to the warmer world outside!
Our patience is spent.
For us your sin is far too great.
Away with you, go outside our gate!
Your hurting means nothing to us now.
To you we show the door.
The door is closed, at once shut tight.
But Heaven's whisper is audible.
The Word is loud and clear,
To all who dare cast others out:
Remember where you came from!
"Yes, yes!" we grumble.
"We came from there but we are made new."
"We are not like we were back then."
"So no, we will not forgive or offer grace."
"We have no patience for what we now are not."
"We need not say we are sorry."
"All we have done our God forgot."
My heart cries out, "Help us Lord!"
Such arrogance is poison.
We must not drink that cup.
The cup we thirst for is the cup of Christ,
The cup of compassion and of life blood spent,
Compassion given up for the lost now found,
And for the found not perfect yet.
Lord, Lord! We cry for mercy.
We need your grace again.
(By Mary Banker Harpt)

A PICTURE IS WORTH A THOUSAND WORDS, BUT WHAT'S THE STORY?

It was a Friday in April 2012, about a year after I began this downward climb. I was looking for something, but I can't remember what. Whatever it was, I had thought it must be stashed under my bed. At the beginning of my search, I found a box of pictures. I pulled the box out from under the bed; I lifted the lid.

You know how it is: You might as well sit down in a comfy chair and settle in for a while. This would take some time. I selected one of the bulging photo envelopes and pulled out the first picture. I smiled and chuckled softly. I pulled out the second picture and turned my head gently from side to side with a barely audible giggle. "They grow up so fast."

At this point, there was no turning back. Whatever I was looking for to begin with was of no pressing importance. My original task, whatever it was, became "a trip down memory lane."

Some of the envelopes in the box were labeled: Alaska, Wedding Shower, Baby Shower, Chequamegon, Christmas, and Birthdays. A few pictures dated back five, ten, and fifteen…as many as forty years. I recalled the hundreds of pictures in an older box that used to be unsorted by any kind of order. This box was mostly of more recent pictures with snapshots of adult children and infant and growing grandchildren. But a few pictures from way back had made their way into this newer time capsule.

I discovered family pictures from a lifetime ago: in one I was standing arm in arm with my ex-husband, and in another, we were seated on the floor in an extended family picture and he was leaning into me. Both of us were smiling. Things were not always as they seemed. There were stories hidden from the camera lens.

After previewing a few pictures, Beth presented something worth pondering: *It is important and helpful to remember the past with dignity and respect.*

She commented, "In the general scheme of things, what do we do with the past? People often think it is an all-or-none situation. They think they have to cut the past off or cut it out. We continue grieving and are left with a bitter taste. It is complicated for people who really loved the one who rejected them or those like Bob with a compartmentalized love. So confusing. Some think, 'The past doesn't mean what I thought it meant.' It is not a death, but making a change for a meaningful present. Childhood and high school friendships end, but we do not desire to cut it out or away. We are all on a journey. How do we honor and respect the time spent? It is a place of sorrow. It is part of the woven fabric. It is not a death, but a change. How do we think about grieving? How do we remember the contributions of the relationship? Of course, the children. And there is more. Does time that has passed lose value in the future?"

Becoming angry is a means of survival in the early stages of a divorce. It allows a person to detach and push away. How does one value and love and detach from one's spouse? If we box the past up and nullify it, it adds to a burden we carry. There is a need for anger sometimes, but it is not where you want to live. It is good to get to a place where you can respect your past and treat a person with dignity and respect as a contributor to your past.

I recalled the times my daughter responded to my positive reflections of the past by saying, "Dad doesn't let himself remember the good things." I once told my son that I wouldn't want any other man to be his father. I can see how I have grown through adversity. I have gained wisdom and understanding and my capacity for compassion has grown, as well as a deeper knowing of myself and of my God.

Now, dear Reader, I am taking us from the crevasse of a mountain to the crevice of a molar in a mouth. A wounded past and the attending hidden and difficult emotions disregarded and ignored become damaging decay that puts the health of heart and mind and soul at risk. I used to be a dental assistant. I put my hands in people's mouths and looked inside. (That is why I floss at least once a day...) In any case, I have seen teeth suffering from decay. It is critical to remove the decay to save the tooth. Sometimes the decay is apparent just by looking at the tooth. Sometimes it is discovered because the doctor examines the tooth with an explorer and can detect a spot where the tough enamel has been destroyed and decay is present. X-rays are needed as well to reveal hidden decay. Laser decay detection provides the ability to get reliable measurements of decay at an early stage. Identifying decay early allows dental professionals to treat cavities while the tooth structure can be preserved. The earlier decay is detected and the tooth is restored, the healthier things are and the less expensive the treatment.

The soft decay must be removed without a trace remaining. The dental professional rinses the tooth and dries the interior and exterior surfaces. The doctor carefully examines the tooth. She sees a small, dark spot there and removes it with a drill piece. When she does this, it is not painful, for she has gently anesthetized that area of the patient's mouth. The dark spot of decay has to be removed. If it is not, decay will continue its destruction and the life of the tooth will remain in jeopardy.

Routine dental check-ups, good oral hygiene, and healthy eating habits are important to oral health. Responding to symptoms and seeing a professional who has the knowledge and skill to identify the problem, shine some light on the sensitive area, and determine steps for restoration are crucial. If the area is left unattended, the decay will worsen, the strength of the tooth will be compromised, the root may be injured, and the tooth will abscess and die. Even then, it can be restored. But it requires telling someone about it, getting needed care, shedding light on it, finding and removing the decay, and restoring the tooth.

The best thing is to brush and floss your teeth. Learn how to take care of them and then follow through! But you and I will always need dentists and hygienists. Even other health conditions can cause injury to our mouths, teeth, and gums. Smoking is evil for teeth, so stop it!

Dental health, physical health, psychological health, spiritual health, relational health and financial health all require care and attention. Consultation with professional specialists is important to good health in all of these areas of human being and well-being, growth and development.

PARTNERING WITH TRAUMA FOR A LONG TIME

So here's the thing. I have been climbing downward for about a year now. I would like to know why I felt what I felt when my ex turned when I said "Hi" to him at an event yesterday. Seeming not to know at first who had offered the greeting, he mumbled, "Hi, Ma…" He didn't quite say "Mary." Why did I feel what I felt just then? I was inserting myself and not accepting being treated as if I were not visible, but something was still awry. The word "awry" came to mind, but does it really fit here? What does "awry" mean anyway? Crooked, askew, twisted, cockeyed, off-center, aslant. Yes, it fits well. Feeling the really "awry" of it all, I said to myself, "I want a glass of wine."

What is up with that?

There were a number of things I wanted to share with Beth at our next session. I had been working on my book, for one thing. I had news that was fun to share about a friend. I had said "Hi" to the old Bob when I saw him and immediately said to myself, "I would like a glass of wine."

I started at the end of the list, knowing this was the deeper part of the crevasse I had to climb into.

"Your brain has learned to have a trauma response, with Bob as the trigger. You have partnered with it for so long… When you think of him, you feel this."

After all I have climbed through, why do I still need soothing in this place?

"It is a place in your head that you went to. When you go there, you like to go there with a glass of wine. This is more about how you feel about yourself."

Here is the discomfort that I want to soothe. I don't like me. The wine helps me to feel more comfortable.

"I sense a self-loathing. I sense a restless agitation that is coming from self-loathing. You really don't like yourself. You can't change it. You can't fix it. You could always fix things, make it right. This is an area where you just can't fix it. You can't make it okay. You reject the brokenness in yourself."

Beth sat with me and took me through a process of recognizing what it was I disliked about myself. I sat back in the chair and closed my eyes. I began to relax and focus on letting myself go to a place where I could identify what it was I did not like about me. I responded out loud, "I *hate* my passivity." At that point, I opened my eyes. I had surprised myself. I was just letting myself go into the place of releasing and finding what it was that we were now uncovering. It was a very powerful and revealing exercise.

If I shared anything with Bob, he would negate what I said. Invalidation would occur once again. He would not respond in a way that lets me be right.

I see that fear in myself, and I am afraid to face it. It drives me crazy. I am not fully free to speak my mind. I want to speak what is right and not need agreement or anything else from the other person. There is more work to do in this crevasse. I hate this loathing feeling. Beth asked what color I would give this feeling. I responded, "Puke pink and brown." If I numb it a little bit, it is more tolerable or avoidable. My performance and my achievements will not rid me of this or overcome it. I hate myself in this place. I have never been strong enough to find the way out.

I need to be mindful that my ex-husband is God's concern, not mine.

And there is the truth that "We all want to cover our weaknesses, one way or another."

I've kissed a snake, for heaven's sake! I am not afraid of snakes anymore. I had asked myself then: what is it that I am afraid of? It seems that we are usually afraid of something. Marty is soft and cuddly, not slimy. I pick him up and hold him. I feed him. I talk to him. He lives in my den, my computer room. So, what is it now that I am afraid of?

I am not afraid of being known anymore. I do not hate snakes anymore. Friends helped me approach snakes. They held my hand. They encouraged me. Professionals showed me that reptiles, including snakes, were not something to dread. They were not something to fear. So I became familiar with snakes. With the nearness of a professional who tended reptiles and understood them, with the nearness of people who loved me, I came to a place where I could hold a snake and even welcome one into my home as a pet.

Likewise, with the guidance of a professional and dear friend, I can face the snake I fear and dread the most: my own passivity. I do hate my passivity and I dread it. I fear that I will relate that way again in a love relationship. (And, wouldn't you know, some particular ministries I have embraced will require me to be an activist.) In this session with Beth, I recognized that I do not have to be afraid of my passivity. I feel as if I have indeed reached the very bottom of the crevasse, and that there is a way out. I will change how I talk to myself and be okay with myself. I do not want to live in fear and I don't want to dislike myself anymore. I will change my behavior and insert myself into the situation. I will make a contribution and not hold back in fear that I will be rejected or misunderstood, disagreed with, or invalidated. I will fear and trust God who loves me and holds me and my destiny in the palm of his hand.

Beth clarified how I have been partnering with the trauma (and passivity) for a long time. I have been swinging with my trauma partner for over forty years and with passivity for most of my life. *Honor your partner. Honor your corner. Swing your partner.* It was kind of like square dancing.

SWING YOUR PARTNER
ROUND'N ROUND

Square dancing grew out of many different yet similar dances from a variety of ancestries, including English, Scandinavian, French, Spanish, and Scottish. In the square dance step called a "swing," partners face each other. *The "Gent" takes one step to the center and alongside the "Lady." The outside of the right feet should touch to start the swing. The left foot is about six inches to the side with the toe of the left foot in line with the heel of the right foot. The dancers take a regular arm position, leaning back a bit to obtain some leverage. With a slight pivot step on the ball of the right foot, the dancers shove themselves around on the left foot as if it were like a scooter. (Mike Dust, Fascinatum! Volume 3- No. 7 Square Dance Term Glossary)*

Yes, the description can get your mind spinning until you apply it point by point. It will make sense and get you swinging as hoped. Now, it is fine to be spun in a square dance in a step and direction you want to go, but I do not need or want a partner that spins me where I do not want to go.

Over twenty years ago, I attended a holiday celebration at the company where George worked. One of the events was a large, group square dance with a professional caller. I soon discovered that there were a number of serious square dancers in the mix. When I was swung by an adept dancer, he would place his hand firmly on my middle back. It felt good. The "gent" was gentle and gracious, confident in his step and solid in his approach. I felt assured that I would be moved in the right direction to complete the swing. I was swinging where I wanted to go. It was a good and safe feeling. I liked it.

When I see my ex-husband and the buried traumatic emotions appear from out of the corner, I inhale the trauma I have partnered with for so long. I am spun until I feel like throwing up. I don't like it, and it sure does not feel safe.

I learned the dance, but I am no longer dancing with my husband. He does not look like the man I knew. I do not know him anymore. I no longer feel the need for him to recognize the trauma and to say he is sorry. He has lost his power over me, and I will not assign him any. I have released the love and self I sacrificed into the caring hands of God, in whom love is never wasted. I have come to know forgiveness and freedom at another level.

Who or what now is spinning me, swinging me around in circles where I do not want to go or be? Is it the trauma I have partnered with for so long that was buried and shared with no one? I also recognize another partner I have paired up with in all of this: my dislike for myself. "If only I had been different or had responded differently or was prettier, my husband would have treated me differently." I hated my passivity and how I let myself be spun out of control in a direction I did not want to go. This is not how the dance of my life goes. Is it that I need to forgive myself? I have weaknesses. I can't perform and achieve myself out of this mess I find myself in. I cannot remove the black spot of dark decay. It is not something that can be soothed away or outdone in achievement.

Are there fears behind my passivity? Does the fear of making a mistake hide there? Does the fear of rejection? Or the fear of confronting, or of being misunderstood? Is my passivity an automatic and instant surrender I acquired over time from never being allowed to be right, no matter what my case? Is it the dread of being invalidated once again without a supportive rescue close by? I want to be done with this. I will not be spun around with trauma now and I won't spin around waiting for someone to say what I want to hear or wait for them to love me again. I will not be in a continual spin of fear. So with enough power or innate strength, with enough of the determination and bold tenacity that I employ for just about everything else, can I take care of the mess?

I will not sit silently by at any opportunity to insert myself and make a difference. I will speak out when the truth needs to be said in a relationship. I will get more and more comfortable and more and more timely and prompt and even immediate in my response. Passivity is a part of my makeup, but it does not define who I am or how I must respond to life and living. I will not live in fear. I will not be spun out of control by a dislike for myself or a paralyzing remembrance of trauma. I will dance with a partner who loves me, adores me, respects me, and appreciates me, values me, and desires my well-being. I will dance my life long with the right partner. And I will dance for eternity with God in my corner and his hand on my back, keeping me safe and spinning me where I want to go and where I want to be: with him forever.

CAUGHT UP IN A SONG AND HOOKED ON A FEELING

I poured myself a cup of coffee and sat down in a comfy chair. I opened my spiral journal, pulled a pen out of my purse pocket, and tried to chase down and record my meandering thoughts as I waited for my scheduled appointment. I was glad to have arrived early. I prayed for the Holy Spirit to fill me up, to fill Beth up. I prayed for the Holy Spirit to be fully present in the learning of the morning.

Some old songs were playing in the lounge. Just then, it was B.J. Thomas singing "Hooked on a Feeling." It is a fun thing how "oldies but goodies" from your youth can trigger the emotions of your youth and how youngness can fill your head. This particular song was and is a song you can get caught up in. "I'm hooked on a feeling that you're in love with me. When you hold me in your arms so tight, you make me know everything's all right…" (composed by Mark James.)

I just had gotten together with a new date referral for coffee and a scone the Friday before. As I listened to "Hooked on a Feeling" that Monday morning, I knew it would be easy and nice to just get dreamy and imagine that the guy I had met on Friday was really going to call me. We could go to a movie or out for dinner and have a dreamy date. He was nice-looking, had a nice voice, and the conversation had been great fun. He closed the coffee rendezvous with one of the similar misleading spiels other guys have used to essentially say, "Nice meeting you, but I won't be calling anytime soon." It was okay if he didn't want to get together again. So I was not the person he wanted to date. Nothing I was going to say or do would make him jump for joy to call me. You see, I was learning about this crazy dance on the over-the-hill dating stage. I had enjoyed meeting him and enjoyed our conversation. It would be nice if the guy would just be above-board and say what he means and mean what he says. I guess it is something we all have to be aware of and work on.

So I did not let myself waste my time on a dead-end daydream, but I did wonder about what feeling I was hooked on in my marriage. I shared my waiting room interlude with Beth and asked, "What is it with me?"

"All of us have this addiction to being un-rejected. Rejection creates a drive to get the rejection to un-rejection. The feeling you were hooked on can be really translated *hooked on un-rejection*. It is an obsession with being un-rejected. We have to undo the rejection in response to the need for that person to love us. In the process, the person, the rejecter, becomes overvalued, idealized, and idolized. The paradox is that at this point, the person may not even like or love the rejecter, yet obsesses about failing."

The drive to be un-rejected will overrule the logical appraisal of the person. It is almost instinctive to strive to be un-rejected and consequently, be obsessed over the person, overvalue, and idealize him.

In the song, *hooked on a feeling* is more about the euphoria of falling in love. The *hooked on a feeling* place I spun around in was a place where I couldn't let go. There is something in our nature, in my nature, which insists on fighting to be accepted.

Beth explained, "An antidote to that deafening insistence is to view the reaction as a form of narcissism, an insistence that everyone like you. 'Why can't I be rejected? I don't have to be liked by everyone. I need to and will stop insisting that everyone like me. I am not likable, lovable, or wanted by everyone, and that is okay.' It is okay not to be wanted, but it is insistence to be wanted that can masquerade as love."

Beth continued, "For you, Mary, your same tenacity and achievement orientation mixes with that drive to be un-rejected and you fight and fight and fight for it. You keep trying to make that happen. It is an insistence that he loved you before and will love you now, again. 'I will figure it out. I will be his everything. I will love what he loves, and I will become what he wants me to be. I will give him anything. I will lose my identity in his personal pursuits.'"

"It is harder when you once captured your husband's imagination and love but now can't accept that you lost it. All things become familiar and all things become old or even annoying. You sustained an injury to the very core of self: 'I once was lovable and now he does not love me.' The person has changed in disposition toward you. You can accept the change or get locked into serving the drive for un-rejection, when all things start to form around this behavior."

My husband loved other women. It does not mean he did not love me at one time. Perhaps he did. I do not think he ever really loved me. His messages were confusing. Perhaps I was the one he chose as his wife, partner, companion, mother of his children. Yet he told me he wanted to be the man to father another woman's child. Perhaps he did. This I do not know.

It was important for me to see and acknowledge the true factor of rejection in my life. To comprehend this propensity to fight against rejection with a cursed desire to be un-rejected was an awakening for me that gets me off the hook and off the hooked-on feeling.

My husband rejected me. The man I had an affair with rejected me. I rejected me. I rejected God. God did not reject me. I did not have to fight for God's love; I don't have to fight to keep it. We have the capacity to love because, and only because, God first loved us. All love comes from God. God's love is perfect love. Human beings are broken and sinful. That brokenness and sinfulness affects our capacity to love and receive love, but there is hope for things to be made new.

20

RETURNING TO THE SCENE OF THE CRIME

About five years after my divorce, I met George. A friend had introduced him to me; he was a friend of her boyfriend. I grew to really care for George; in fact, I fell in love with him. One day I was amazed to realize that I could love another man as much as I had loved my ex-husband. We spent a lot of time together. We went running and biking together. He included me in events at his company. At their employee Christmas party, all the kids received gifts and each family received a beautiful Christmas tree. They also took pictures of couples and families, and George wanted me to pose with him and his three children for their photo. It was lovely. I thought I looked pretty. Sometime in March 1989, we separated over a disagreement. I felt that he could not comprehend or appreciate how very important my children are to me. During that time of separation, God got my attention.

Go back with me now, six years earlier, December 1983: I didn't remember how I had explained the loss of the clay figurine to my three children during Christmas time in 1983. I did not confess to them that I had thrown the manger out the front door one night.

The snow melted and spring arrived. Time passed. I graduated from college with honors, landed a job, and launched a great career. I lifted weights, ran races, biked, and competed in more triathlons. I crossed many finish lines. I had fallen in love with George but, for the time being, had broken off the relationship. A close friend and co-worker disappeared in December of 1988. His body was found in the Milwaukee River on April 25th, 1989. He had been murdered. [His death remains an unsolved mystery to this day.]This good and amazing man was greatly loved by his wife, family, and the YMCA family. His life, death, and the words spoken at his funeral made a powerful impact on my being.

After those six years of intensely racing for multiple finish lines, I ran out of myself. On May 3rd, 1989, a pastor, a good friend and volunteer for the YMCA, asked if I would join him for lunch. As we waited for our food, he said to me, "Mary, you matter to God." Then this prayer warrior pulled the still-folded white dinner napkin aside, took a pen from his suit coat pocket, and began to chicken-scratch out a diagram of the meaning of the Gospel to make clear the truth of the Cross. That night, God was clearly convicting me that I had messed up in many ways.

I did not like the bitterness in my life. I didn't want to feel like that anymore. I was sorry for what I had become and for what I had done. I wanted to change. The next morning, I dropped my Joy off at the high school. As she stepped out of the car and turned to say good-bye, I said to her, "I think I want Jesus in my life." I wasn't sure what was happening. I went back to the house and picked up Katy and John and dropped them off at their grade school. On the way home, at 8:00 in the morning, May 4, 1989, alone in my dark blue Tempo and turning into our neighborhood before heading off to work, I was talking. "God, I am sorry. I don't want to be like this anymore. God, I want you back in my life."

And nothing has been the same since. Here I am, one who once doubted. The one who threw out the baby Jesus with the manger, now has him living in her heart. Jesus can show up and penetrate granite.

The New Nativity and my adorable cat Gideon

I have chosen the way of truth; I have set my heart on your laws. I hold fast to your statutes O LORD; do not let me be put to shame. I run in the path of your commands, for you have set my heart free. (Psalm 119:30–32 NIV)

Fully embracing the message of the Cross, realizing I desperately needed Jesus, and hearing that I matter to him was the combination to the lock that opened the door to the prison of my soul. Following this conversion experience, I reconnected with George, and he soon asked me to marry him. We picked out a beautiful ring. It was perfect. We went together to see a builder to buy a lot and picked out a plan for a beautiful house in a lovely area of the city. I was a single mom working for what he called "missionaries' pay." He, of course, paid cash for the lot and the house.

After all of this, I found myself standing at a crossroads. I Corinthians 6:14 and Jeremiah 6:16 waged battle in my mind and in my heart. George was agnostic. He said, "You believe what you believe and I believe what I believe. It makes no difference. If it works for you," he would contend, "that's okay. In five years, it will probably fade and you will be on to something else." For him, life simply came down to "can you buy a refrigerator or not?" Yet, he had shared with me that he had always thought that when he earned his first million, he would have arrived. That would be "it." But he soon learned that it wasn't it, nor was becoming a multimillionaire. Still it wasn't enough. Something was still missing.

I really wanted to marry George. It was so absolutely wonderful to be held by someone again and to be loved and cared for. I loved and cared for him deeply.

But there was a restlessness. I wasn't sure what it meant not to be at peace about something, but that was where I was. Something just wasn't right in my plans to marry George. Something so seemingly simple, like praying at the dinner table, would become a dividing issue. I remembered one evening when we were watching TV at my home with all of the kids. I caught myself saying, "I am going to be alone again." That is what I was feeling, but at the moment I did not know why. I actually said it softly out loud, not meaning to. I was startled by what I said. I became more and more confused whether I should marry George or not. I had asked others for their input and became even more confused.

One evening, I was particularly restless about the whole thing. Enabled by God's grace and in his tender mercy and patience, I surrendered the decision to him. I actually was lying face down on my dining room floor. I was pounding on the carpeted floor as I said, "I don't understand this. I don't understand any of this." I then got up and walked into the living room. I went down on my knees as I finished my sentence: "Yet nevertheless, let your will be done." Just as I was formulating my thoughts, somewhere between and mixed in the place where thoughts and words meld, as my knees just touched the floor, the message was clear. *You cannot marry George.*

"Oh. Well, okay then." I got up as quickly as I had gotten down on my knees and knew without a shadow of a doubt that I could not marry George.

Days later I said to myself, "I certainly would not be showing love to George, if I married him and in so doing was telling him that a relationship with God really didn't matter."

Initially, I had thought God had taken me to this crossroads immediately following my conversion experience to test the depths and devotion of my decision, to do a heart-check. Later I realized that God was providing an opportunity for me to more fully comprehend how much I loved him and to embrace how much he means to me in my life and in my living. God loved me. He never rejected me. I found my true identity in him.

God had taken all of my mess, including my failure to be authentic, my idolization of my husband, and my poisonous affair, to show me what my human nature was like separated from him. I saw myself in a mirror of truth. I saw what I looked like apart from the grace of God. In God's great grace, I was redeemed and restored. Returning to the scene of the crime of throwing God out of my life, it was obvious that I was the criminal. Jesus paid the penalty and I was set free from the prison of my own making.

And now, during this journey into the crevasse, I understood the thoughts and emotions behind what I had said so many years before when I was in my living room and watching television with my children, my fiancé George, and his children. "I am going to be alone again." I now understand that I had finally found myself again over the first six years following my divorce and realized I would risk losing it again if I married George. I felt this awful dread that I would forfeit myself and relinquish my identity again. I actually thought life would get harder. When I asked God back into my life, I had discovered the fullness of my identity in him and in a relationship with him. I would not and will not forfeit myself again, so help me, God!

I dated throughout the six years following my divorce. After I ended the relationship with George, I said, "Ok, God. If you want me to get married again, you are going to have to take the guy, plop him down in front of me, and say, *Here!*"

21

REFLECTIONS ON RADICAL REDEMPTION

My four-year-old granddaughter had been busy making things for lunch, including tea and a number of tasty dishes. She would carry the completed delicacies and set them on the table where I was sitting. I would then comment on how very delicious the food was, and the tea, especially tasty. She would then return to the sandbox and prepare some more yummy things for me to taste and enjoy.

She was not at all bothered by Boaz, who would continuously drop the now-saliva-drippy-and-sand-gritty-not-so-yellow tennis ball in the sandbox by her adorable four-year-old feet. She would patiently pick up the ball and throw it without even looking up. Sometimes she would stand up and give the ball a good toss. Bo kept retrieving the ball and bringing it back to her. The interruptions in her cooking did not seem to bother her. After a while, she did remark, "Bo, go find something else to do."

When we went back into the house and I removed my sandals, she looked at my bare feet and pondered for a moment. "Grandma, you have old feet." Then, looking at her own very cute feet she added, "You should get some new ones like mine."

New feet would be nice. It would be quite lovely if I could go to the *Creation Store* and redeem my old feet for a pair of beautiful young feet. While I was there, I would stop in at the skin-renewal department and convert my wrinkly skin to soft, very soft, baby-like skin. I would then exchange my puffy stomach for my younger, tight abdominal muscles. It would be quite fun to redeem my old body for a new one.

Actually, that will be the case at the end of times here on earth, when all who believe in Jesus Christ will receive a new body. And when you open the door to your heart to let the waiting and ready Jesus enter in and take up residence there, the Bible says, we become a new creation. I have to say that when I asked God into my life, it felt like my heart was indeed set free. I have shared some of the stories of my life journey on the road to healing and forgiveness. It is profitable to ponder the process.

My prayer in my car back in 1989, a prayer of Holy Spirit-enabled surrender, freed me from bitterness, restored my relationship with God, and gave me new life. Eight years later, I was riding off-road in the Northern Kettles with Jesus as my companion. The off-road bike ride and communion with Jesus at the lake gave me freedom and hope in knowing I was known, understood, loved, and valued by Jesus. He knew and understood my story; he knew and wanted to lift my burdens and relieve my hurting and sorrow. He was always and forever with me.

And here is another wedding dress story, four years after the great ride and my oldest daughter's wedding day. I was sitting in the driver's seat, in my car, in my garage. I sat at the wheel; the keys were still in my hand. I felt as if I did not have the strength to put the keys in the ignition. I sighed and thought, *I can't do this. I cannot do this again.* Then my thoughts moved to prayer. "God I cannot go through this again, I cannot go to this gathering to look at wedding dresses now for Katy. She (my ex-husband's wife) will be there, and she is someone I wish would not be there. I just hate this. I just can't do this, God. I can't drive there and do this. I need a miracle." And God delivered.

I started the car and drove to the bridal salon. The evening spent with my dear daughter as she tried on many wedding dresses was miraculously light, fun, and enjoyable. God had lifted the heaviness and sorrow that had always attended gatherings where my ex-husband and/or his wife were present. The feelings that were lifted for that event remained on the sidelines for over a decade. I had felt relief for about the past ten years. It was as if a pressure valve had been opened and all the awfulness escaped.

Yes, there was much growth and life and living that happened in and around all of these years gone by. Now, at this time, ten years after the wedding dress miracle and twenty-two years after God penetrated granite in 1989, I discovered that healing and forgiveness needed to go deeper still. *There was something there that had a hold on me, because I was holding onto something.* The dungeon had been blown apart. The jail door was opened and the prisoner set free, yet she remained in a stronghold that had a stranglehold on her authentic self.

There were stages of relief and release. Forgiveness and healing were processes with platforms of healing and growth infused with love, mercy, grace, and hope, one as significant and meaningful as the other. God redeemed my life in more ways than I could ever have imagined.

Are affairs a sin against those we love and a sin against God? Yes, they are. Do they cause damage that ruins relationships and grieves the very heart of God? Yes, yes, and yes! God compares his love for us to being the husband of the church. Read the book of Hosea in the Old Testament of the Bible and feel God's pain. Take a look into the heart of God and weep. I was guilty. I let myself love another. But my God, who hates the betrayals of husband and wife, who hates verbal, emotional, sexual, and physical abuse of any measure, is an overcoming God. Even though I had trashed my German Bible, I had thrown out the baby Jesus with the manger, and I had relinquished my values and beliefs; he turned my awfulness into new beginnings. After I abandoned God and forfeited myself in my marriage, God in his great mercy and grace offered me new life. While I still rejected him, he began his rescue of me and initiated redemption of my life. He resurrected my buried talents and dreams. He let me "come alive again." I was important to him. He still wanted me to become his daughter.

The Lord sets the prisoners free. (Psalm 146: 7 ESV)

God was doing these things even though I spit in his face. He held out an offer too good to refuse. "Come to me and I will give you rest. Cast all your cares upon me. This is the reason I came: to seek and save the lost." (Paraphrased from Matthew 11:28, Psalm 55:22, and from Luke 19:10.)

God was looking after me when I was a child. He walked by me while I was in school and pursuing excellence in the areas I felt wired for, called to do. I find it amazing that even when I forsook him, he did not forget about me. I threw out my German Bible, his story. I threw it in the garbage. Yet he did not consider me refuse. I was salvageable. He would make me into something brand new. The heavenly Potter, working with this lump of clay deformed by my choices, actions, and failure to act, was making something new. My pride was in the mix along with my failure to realize just how much I needed rescue. I needed a Savior. I couldn't cut it on my own. My selfishness and sin, my fears and my frailties were wretched. I had broken the heart of God and he was willing and waiting to put mine back together.

Even after I threw out his Word and launched the baby Jesus, God was planning for my return. He was patient, longsuffering, and overflowing with mercy and grace. He was waiting for Mary to come back to him and to be made brand new. He was waiting for his prodigal daughter to get off her self-made mountain of delusion, fall on her knees, and ask him to come into her life. His hand was on the doorknob he had already turned to open; so I just had to push the door and let him in, into the mess I had made. In my broken state of mind, body, and soul, he was waiting for me to come to him and say, "Please forgive me, Father. I have sinned. I want you in my life. Please fix me and make me whole and complete in you."

God not only redeemed my life, he redeemed the dreams I myself had forfeited. Why should he give me a second chance? Why should he be so good to me? Why should he love me like he does? Not because of me or anything I do, that's for sure. He is merciful and he is full of grace. In time, God fulfilled all my dreams in ways far greater than I ever imagined:

June 1952: I was born.

June 1970: Graduated from High School

September 1970–December 1971: Completed three semesters of college

July 1971: Married

July 1972: Joy was born.

December 1974: Katy was born.

July 1980: John was born.

March 1981: Started running

June 1981: First Triathlon

September 1981: Tinman Triathlon

April 1982: Marital separation

May 1982: Returned to college

March 1983: Received award for Outstanding Academic Achievement

October 1983: Divorced

1983: Threw out the baby Jesus

January 1984: Recruited by YMCA as a Strength Training Coach

1985: Elected to Phi Beta Kappa

December 1985: Received Bachelor of Arts (cum laude)

1986: Began professional career with YMCA

December 1988: Close friend and co-worker disappeared. Just before his disappearance he had talked with me about God.

April 1989: My friend's body was discovered. The message at his funeral touched me greatly.

May 4, 1989: When I was the least lovable, a friend told me I mattered to God. I asked God back into my life, and nothing has been the same since.

November 1989: Ended the engagement with George

1989: Traveled to Honduras on a YMCA and Eyeglass Mission

1991: Traveled to the Philippines on a YMCA and Eyeglass Mission

1994: I served as a representative of the Milwaukee YMCAs at the 13th World Council in London, the birthplace of the YMCA. One thousand leaders representing over 100 nations gathered in London to commemorate the 150th Anniversary of the YMCA.

1994: After attending the World Council of YMCAs, I traveled on my own to Germany for five days. I saw all of the places I had dreamed about for so many years. I was able to converse auf Deutsch with local Germans on the plane, trains, and daily adventures.

2006–2010: Traveled on Mission trips to Sudan, Kenya, Tanzania, Belize, and Moldova

October 2006: Went mountain climbing for the first time

November 2006: Retired from a beautiful and rewarding career with the YMCA

December 19, 2006, 9:10 a.m.: Summited Mount Kilimanjaro

December 2007: Received my Masters in Theology

March 5, 2011: Taken to the edge of the crevasse and began the downward climb to freedom

2011-2012: Wrote and published a book

All of the many goals and dreams that I had worked toward and hoped for were within my grasp in high school. I had released them one by one for the sake of my relationship with Bob. God redeemed them all. Since 1983, I have visited over fifteen different countries, including Germany. God made a way for my three children to be my very best friends. I have friends around the world and in many states. I have reconnected with friends from high school and have developed many treasured friendships throughout my career and in my church involvement. I had let go of all my friends during high school. I once again have so many wonderful friends, including people I loved in the workplace for so many years. At my recent fortieth high school reunion, I was back with the friends I had let go of. A number of years ago, God reconnected me with another old high school friend and it has been wonderful. I saw and had a long conversation with my dear friend and debate coach at the reunion. The reunion event was magical. In multiple areas of my life and around the world, I am blessed with many friends. My license plate letters once included my initials and the first initials of my children. They were and are my best friends. Now, I have found a way to include and represent my kids, their spouses and all the grandkids in my license plate letters.

My life was enriched with the opportunity to participate in life in many different occupational roles from winding the guides on fishing rods for $1.10 an hour at age fourteen to managing one of the finest YMCAs in the country.

I had the great gift to visit and thoroughly enjoy three places I had always wanted to visit: Germany, Alaska, and the Grand Canyon. Many of my travels have included one or more of my children. Those adventures were all indeed magical. All of my travels have included dear friends. I could go on and on about the amazing adventures we have had together. I earned a bachelor's and a master's degree, dreams of mine since I was a little kid. (I think I am on the road to earning a PhD in Downward Climbs.) I have noted how I turned down a sought-after scholarship when I was in high school; I was awarded another (albeit a small one) when I returned to college. I have served as a missionary in a number of countries and in the workplace. I have been granted many opportunities to preach to groups both large and small. I have had a multitude of opportunities to encourage people in many arenas of my life, in one-on-one connections and through my writing from sticky notes to letters, emails, and texts, as well as longer works of the heart.

I have noted how on Mother's Day in 1989, following my conversion experience, my kids gave me an NIV Study Bible. I found myself reading Psalm 119. Verses 30–32 became my life verse, which has always found its way onto the back of my business cards. The Bible, once discarded, has found its way to my desk in the den, to the kitchen table, to my favorite recliner in the living room, to my bedside table, to the front seat of my car, to my desk at work, to the prisons I have visited, to the Roof of Africa, to the ancient ruins of Ephesus and Pergamum, and to planes, trains, and automobiles around the world.

During my recent journey to authenticity, I looked for a German Bible for my granddaughters, who were attending a German Immersion School (and for their mom and dad, of course). I found the ESV Parallel Bible with German and English side by side. I bought one for my granddaughters and family, one for my mother and father, and one for me. I didn't realize until I turned the pages and read Psalm 139 in German that this new Bible was the same translation I had read those many years ago. Psalm 139 once again offered great comfort and encouragement for me (of course, it's on my webpage business card). It was a soul-reviving experience to be able to read through and pray this Psalm in German as I had a long time ago in the darkest time of my life, in our second apartment. Now God had put this book back into my hands and I could use it when I prayed about those dark years as I visited my old neighborhoods on the journey downward. I got my life back, and my God took me back.

I have had the grand opportunity to give Bibles to a number of people here and around the world. My 1989 Mother's Day gift Bible was getting quite worn. With a bookstore gift card from my staff, I purchased a similar Bible and had the kids reenter their gift note. Years later, I gave this leather Bible to prisoners on death row in Belize and shared the preciousness of it all with them. I was given a Bible in Swahili from good friends in Kenya after we had climbed Kili together. I was given and have given Spanish Bibles to those who wanted to read the Story. I gave Bibles in Romanian to friends in Moldova. Even though I had thrown out the Bible, God let me embrace his-story again and share the Bible beyond expectation.

Remember how I had chosen not to go on my long-awaited band trip in my senior year? God even redeemed that dream. I had played the saxophone; my son studied it, too, and even used my old instrument. He also joined his high school band and went on the band trip. When he returned, he shared his story with me: "Mom, it's almost 11:00 p.m. and I am not even half done." I really wanted a cup of hot herbal tea to sip and enjoy while I listened to his story, but I didn't want to interrupt and maybe lose the moment. How rich and very kind of God was that? Though I had forfeited my own high school band trip, I was granted the rich opportunity to hear about my son's trip and thereby enjoy it right along with him.

All the time and in so many ways, I saw God's great working (and working out) of things. He invested so much attention in me to shape me and mold me. I am sixty years old. He did all of this work just for me? Yes, and he works hard for each and every child, woman, and man. God is an overcoming God, and he is amazing. His healing work doesn't stop there; it keeps on going as we work to share with and encourage others. God is great and he is good.

During the past year, I have heard many stories, many heart cries, where women and men needed someone to listen so they may be known and begin a journey of healing and new beginnings. God has given me grace to listen and to encourage. Any stories of success and achievement, any accounts of survival in difficult circumstances, any Mary "comeback" moments, any rebounds from failure and flops, any working through of injuries and woundedness, are only because of a great and good God who has surrounded me with his love and caring, as well as the listening ears and caring hearts of others. He is our God, an "R" God. He is our God of rescue, revival, restoration, redemption, righteousness, and the purest reality of un-rejection. He is the Rock on which we can stand.

God was and is a redeeming God in the throes and aftermath of adversity. *He used the adversity I encountered to reveal my true self and the true Jesus, giving way to a true faith.*

It is a great compelling for me to write. It is a life assignment God set before me. I write in response to his leading in my life. I write to reach out and help out. I open up my life to lift up others. I reveal my woundedness and I expose my shame so that others, too, might see the healing benefit in being known and the awareness that our stories have similar themes. I was broken and God put me back together. I pour out my stories in the process of spilling out myself so others might venture to open their minds and hearts and wounded pasts, exposing them to the healing hand of God. The fullness of this healing requires me and likewise requires all of us to be known by others.

In her powerful and best-selling classic, *The Verbally Abusive Relationship*, Patricia Evans writes, "It takes tremendous self-esteem to validate one's own reality when no one else seems to have done so. Sometimes, just a book that describes it, or knowing that one person 'out there' understands can make all the difference." (p. 63) It is my humble prayer that *The Downward Climb* will serve such a purpose and that others will feel understood, validated, and valued.

Through it all and above all, it is my desire that you know God loves you and that you matter to him. He knows your story. He understands and he is here. Out of the crevasse we rise, healed and whole in the arms of our Father.

22

YOUR BOOTS ARE THE MOST IMPORTANT THING WHEN YOU ARE CLIMBING MOUNTAINS

Your boots are the most important thing when you are climbing mountains. When you are gearing up and working out to prepare to climb to the Roof of Africa, your boots are the most critical piece of your gear. It is essential to take great pains to get the right boots and the right size in order to avoid great pains on your climb. It is more than wise to wear them and break them in prior to your trip up the mountain.

I did the research. Check it out: Boot height, weight, waterproofing, breathability, support, durability, uppers, outsoles, insoles, size, fit, and comfort. I shopped. I asked the experts. I tried many on and tried some out. When I learned about and saw the pair I eventually selected, I had a good feeling it might be the one. I thought the boots were almost jumping off the high shelf right into my arms. When I tried on these very fine boots in the right size, I knew I had found the ones for me. The price point was higher than others I had looked at and tried on; but when it came to my boots, I was going to get the right ones at any cost. I tried them out on the trails in Wisconsin. Nice. Yes, very nice. I wore my boots on the plane. I might lose all of my suitcases, but my boots were going with me to Africa.

New Boots for Kili Climb December 2006

On our climb, the Kenyan guide said to me, "Mary, you have good boots. You need to trust your boots. Put your confidence in your boots. Plant your boot, step up, and lock your knee. If you step on a loose rock, you will stand firm even if the rock is wet. The climb is steep, and you will stand firm."

It was dark when we started our final climb to the summit. I walked right behind our guide with my headlamp shining on his heels and the ground right by my feet. I watched every step he took and planted my boot where he had just lifted his up. Others followed right behind me. Our guide set the pace; he knew how to lead us so we would reach the summit.

For six beautiful and brutal days I climbed Mount Kilimanjaro. My boots took a beating. They took a beating for my feet and delivered endurance for the climb.

Boots That Took a Beating to the Summit and Back Down Again December 2006

For mountain climbing and adventures I had to search for the right boots. For living life and facing adversity, I didn't know what I was looking for, what I needed; but when I *found* God, I knew he was the perfect fit. I was excited to find him, the right one, after a long, long search. I had tried things that didn't work, fell apart, or made me fall apart. I now take God with me on every life excursion, including getting out of bed in the morning. I have good boots, and I have a good and great God. I can trust God. When I take a step or make a move, I can be confident when I plant my life in God. He will lead me to the summit. Whether a particular trail on my life journey is smooth or rough, dry or slippery, I will stand firm. If I slip, he will be my trekking poles to support me and keep me upright. When it is dark, he will be the light that guides my way; I can trust him and follow him step by step.

My God took a beating to take me to the summit of life and living. He loves me and I love him. I won't board the plane without my boots, and I won't make a move without my God.

Rainbow of Hope and Promise over the Trail on Kilimanjaro 2006

EPILOGUE

It was 5:00 pm on Friday, and I was making a fresh salad of home grown tomatoes and cucumbers, fresh spinach leaves, sweet yellow peppers, store fresh mushrooms, a splash of olive oil and a sprinkle of salt. I tore open the mushroom package and began to wash the mushrooms. After I washed the first one, I popped it in my mouth. I continued to rinse the mushrooms and selected a few to slice up and place on the spinach leaves. And then it happened, an unexpected flashback and an immediate response. I bent over, placed my folded arms on the kitchen counter and put my head face down. I exhaled with a heavy sigh.

The process of simply washing the mushrooms stimulated a memory pushed way down. I can't remember the name or face of Bob's mistress I refer to as *Australia*; but when I was the *Young Mary*, she was over at the apartment on Beloit Road. My husband invited her over for dinner, and she brought the fixings for a salad, including mushrooms. I had never had fresh mushrooms before, so she was instructing me on how to prepare them. (Since then I have learned that it is more nutritious to prepare the mushrooms another way. Ha!) Then another buried memory sprang up alongside this demoralizing one. I recalled how my husband and I went out of town with his mistress Rita to meet her family in her childhood home. Her parents and some of her eight siblings were there. Then I remembered the bar scene at the small airport where my husband kept his plane. I had a drink at the bar with Bob. His friend Butch was there and Bob's last mistress. She stirred Butch's brandy and water with her finger. I didn't remember what she said as she stirred the drink. I just remembered the scene.

In our most recent conversation, Beth mentioned the alarming trail of public shaming incidents in my manuscript. The accounts prompted probing questions: *How did I respond? What did I say to Bob? What did I tell myself?* In the downward climb, many questions were answered; I learned a lot. No, I was not at the bottom of the crevasse. Beth once again shared that this was not going to be easy. It would be depressing to sit still with the glaring and flagrant exposure of public shame and my acquiescent response. And days later, as I prepared a salad for dinner, more memories were made manifest

Another summer "memory workout" session with Beth brought a great gift of learning about the challenge to come through the downward climb as a friend of myself, independent of others evaluation of me. My greatest ally is the Holy Spirit; the next in line is me. It is imperative that I am my own ally. "Find yourself, accept yourself, embrace yourself, love yourself, justify yourself. Give yourself permission to be less than ideal." To be an ally for myself is to know myself including flaws and strengths. It is to see myself as I am and embrace myself as God embraces me. The downward climb in part was about finding myself, accepting myself, and becoming my own ally. I don't need to strive to please others in order to gain their acceptance. Their satisfaction was not and is not my assignment in this life.

I was still learning and discovering more freedom.

I had already submitted my manuscript for publication. Just when I thought I must be done, more disturbing memories made themselves known and new experiences triggered old trauma. I did not invite the memories into my present moment, nor did I intend to feel another un-welcome sting of shame and distress. I could go back and insert the epi-sodes of recall, new experiences, and learning into a related part of the submitted script; yet, that isn't how it worked or how the process usually works. Memory does not trace a chronological or linear trail. It is like climbing a mountain with switchbacks and long climbs going up to ac-climatize and heading back down again. There can be multiple false summits, when you think you are nearing the top of the mountain only to realize you have much more to climb before you reach the highest peak. The story unfolds, takes twists and turns, backs up, hangs on a cliff, jerks forward, trips backward, recovers footing and moves forward again.

The weather can change quickly on a mountain top; you never know when a storm might appear. When a life storm from the past shows up in the present, it can send you running down the mountain. During the climb, another life climber might slip and hang perilously over the edge. You stop the climb, reach out your hand and pull the other mountain trekker to safety. You help each other stand up. You catch your breath as you realize how grand it was of God to get you to this place on your life journey just at the right time to help another "mountain explorer."

The interweaving of memories, therapeutic dialogue, storytelling and re-telling, journal writing and journal reading, praying through the journals, listening to the stories of others, and inputting the story on the computer was like weaving a complex silk tapestry with threads of many colors. The weave goes back and forth and back and forth with the picture gradually becoming known. The life tapestry is not completed. There are more memory threads to spin. There is more learning to weave in. There are new stories to begin.

We do not *get over* the wounding of the past. We go through it, but we do not remain in it. We grow stronger and wiser, more gentle and humble. We grow in grace, caring, and compassion. We become authentically human. We learn that we matter to God and find our identity in him. There is life to enjoy and new freedoms to find. (By the way, I did finish making my salad. It was absolutely delicious; I enjoyed every bite of it.)

It is clear that there is a need to *go deeper still.* And there are essential conversations for us to have with God, ourselves, and others for encouragement and endurance on *The Downward Climb.*

Mary Banker Harpt

NOTES

Psalm 18:35 New American Standard Bible

You have also given me the shield of Your salvation,
And Your right hand upholds me;
And Your gentleness makes me great.

Psalm 139:1-18 English Standard Version

O Lord, you have searched me and known me!
² You know when I sit down and when I rise up;
   you discern my thoughts from afar.
³ You search out my path and my lying down
   and are acquainted with all my ways.
⁴ Even before a word is on my tongue,
   behold, O Lord, you know it altogether.
⁶ Such knowledge is too wonderful for me;
   it is high; I cannot attain it.
⁷ Where shall I go from your Spirit?
   Or where shall I flee from your presence?
⁸ If I ascend to heaven, you are there!
   If I make my bed in Sheol, you are there!
⁹ If I take the wings of the morning
   and dwell in the uttermost parts of the sea,
¹⁰ even there your hand shall lead me,
   and your right hand shall hold me.
¹¹ If I say, "Surely the darkness shall cover me,
   and the light about me be night,"

[12] even the darkness is not dark to you;
　　the night is bright as the day,
　　for darkness is as light with you.
[13] For you formed my inward parts;
　　you knitted me together in my mother's womb.
[14] I praise you, for I am fearfully and wonderfully made.[a]
Wonderful are your works;
　　my soul knows it very well.
[15] My frame was not hidden from you,
when I was being made in secret,
　　intricately woven in the depths of the earth.
[16] Your eyes saw my unformed substance;
in your book were written, every one of them,
　　the days that were formed for me,
　　when as yet there was none of them.
[17] How precious to me are your thoughts, O God!
　　How vast is the sum of them!
[18] If I would count them, they are more than the sand.
　　I awake, and I am still with you.

Lamentations 3:19-24　New International Version

I remember my affliction and my wandering,
　　the bitterness and the gall.
[20] I well remember them,
　　and my soul is downcast within me.
[21] Yet this I call to mind
　　and therefore I have hope:
[22] Because of the Lord's great love we are not consumed,
　　for his compassions never fail.
[23] They are new every morning;
　　great is your faithfulness.

²⁴ I say to myself, "The Lord is my portion;
  therefore I will wait for him."

Psalm 119: 30-32 New International Version

I have chosen the way of truth; I have set my heart on your laws. I hold fast to your statutes; O LORD; do not let me be put to shame. I run in the path of your commands, for you have set my heart free.

A FEW OF MANY HAPPY
CHILDHOOD RECOLLECTIONS

There are many moments to recall of my happy childhood, many amazing stories to tell that would show you how wonderful my parents are and how they impacted my life. I received a consistent message of being loved and valued. Through their example of gentleness, fairness, goodness, and the creation of a secure and safe environment, I learned a respect for authority. I knew the authority figures in my life had my well-being at heart. I was exposed to their servant's hearts, their humility and encouraging style in how they interacted with all those around them. They were trustworthy and consistent in their responses, reliable and safe, so I grew up with a strong sense of security. Because of their sensitive parenting, I was given responsibilities appropriate for my age. Through my mother and father, I learned an appreciation for education and an appreciation and respect for God's created world. My brother and sister were great friends. The three of us enjoyed each other's company and companionship. We still do.

Many teachers, including those in Sunday school and especially my high school debate coach, greatly influenced my life. God, in his sovereignty and grace, placed me in the care of these beautiful people and put others in my world to influence my life and my living. I had a very happy childhood, and I knew how wonderful that was from when I was little.

When I decided I wanted to learn how to play the saxophone in third grade, Mom took me to a music store to rent an instrument. I took one look at the keys and felt discouraged. "Mom, I'm not so sure I can do this. It looks awful hard."

Mom said, "Give yourself time. It's not as hard as it looks." She taught me not to give up before I even tried.

BIBLIOGRAPHY

Byock, Ira, M.D. *The Four Things That Matter Most: A Book About Living.* New York: Free Press, 2004.

Dust, Mike. *Mike Dust, Fascinatum! Volume 3- No. 7 Square Dance Term Glossary.* *www.mikedust.com/fascinatum/2003.*

Evans, Patricia. *The Verbally Abusive Relationship.* Massachusetts: Adams Media, 2010.

Green, Dan and Mel Lawrenz. *Encountering Shame and Guilt.* Grand Rapids: Baker Books, 1994.

Nouwen, Henri J.M. *The Inner Voice of Love: A Journey Through Anguish to Freedom.* New York: Doubleday, 1996.

Osborne, Grant R. *Revelation: Baker Exegetical Commentary on the New Testament.* Grand Rapids: Baker Academic, 2002.

Scazzero, Geri and Peter Scazzero. *I Quit!: Stop Pretending Everything Is Fine and Change Your Life.* Grand Rapids: Zondervan, 2010.

Simpson, Joe. *Touching the Void.* New York: Harper Collins, 2004.

Die Bibel/The Holy Bible, English Standard Version, Parallel Bible. Wheaton: Crossway and Stuttgart: Deutsche Bibelgesellschaft, 2009.

The Holy Bible: Updated New American Standard Bible. Grand Rapids: Zondervan, 1995.

NIV / The Message Parallel Bible. Grand Rapids: Zondervan, 2004.

The NIV Study Bible: New International Version. Grand Rapids: Zondervan Publishing House, 1985.

Webster's Ninth New Collegiate Dictionary. Springfield: Merriam-Webster, 1983.

Wikipedia: The Free Encyclopedia at Wikipedia.org.